Asian Words of Success

Thoughts, quotations and phrases on

leadership, marketing and

personal development

from Asia's leading thinkers.

By

Steven Howard

Foreword by Alex Chan

Asian Words of Success

ISBN: 978-1-943702-04-6 (Print edition)
978-1-943702-05-3 (Kindle edition)

For reprint permission, please contact:
Steven Howard
c/o Caliente Press
1775 E Palm Canyon Drive, Suite 110-198
Palm Springs, CA 92264
U.S.A
Email: stevenhoward@verizon.net

Published by:
Caliente Press
1775 E Palm Canyon Drive, Suite 110-198
Palm Springs, CA 92264
U.S.A.
Email: CalientePress@verizon.net

Cover Design: Lee Chee Yih

Asian Words of Wisdom Series

The *Asian Words of Wisdom* series comprises the following titles:

Asian Words of Success — *Thoughts, quotations and phrases on leadership, marketing and personal development from Asia's leading thinkers.*

Asian Words of Meaning — *Reflections and thoughts on success, self-understanding and spiritual guidance from Asia's leading thinkers.*

Asian Words of Inspiration — *Thoughts, motivational quotes and wisdom from Asia's leading thinkers on personal and professional success and the journey of life.*

The Book of Asian Proverbs — *Unabridged collection of ancient sayings and teachings from across Asia.*

Indispensable Asian Words of Knowledge — *Words of wisdom from Asia's leading sages, philosophers, and statesmen.* (October 2016)

Asian Words of Success

Dedication

This book is dedicated to

Haris Manaf

My former colleague and protégé.

Followed his own path to success,

while staying true to his beliefs and values.

That's true success. And admirable.

Well done, professor.

Table of Contents

Asian Words of Success

Introduction

People around the world have long turned to the writings and teachings of Asia's leading thinkers for insights on self-awareness, personal development, virtue, the importance of the family, and the need for continuous cultivation of knowledge.

Today, the words and thoughts of Asian leaders — both past and present — can also teach the West and the East vital lessons in leadership, mentorship, coaching, continuous learning, and the cultivation of solid corporate cultures.

Quotations have always had the power to inspire me. When I was a child I started a collection of quotes on 3x5 index cards, and kept them filed in my own personal plastic box. Ever since I have been a collector of quotes, particularly during my 21 year tenure living in Asia.

Within *Asian Words of Success* you will find over 600 motivational quotations and phrases from some of Asia's leading thinkers: Buddha, Confucius, Gandhi, Jiddu Krishnamurti, Konosuke Matsushita, Lao-Tzu, Sun Tzu, and others.

Asian Words of Success

While we believe all of our sources for these quotations to be reliable, readers should not interpret *Asian Words of Success* as a highly researched, authoritative reference book. This is not what we set out to do and it is certainly not what we have delivered.

What we have set out to do is gather and share the quotes that moved us, impressed us, or got us thinking a bit harder, deeper, or even more lightly. In achieving this endeavor, we trust you will agree, *Asian Words of Success* does deliver.

While technically the continent of Asia extends all the way west to Turkey, most people today seem to cut Asia off at the western border of Pakistan. In truth, the boundaries of Asia are more culturally determined that geographic lines on maps and globes. As such, I have elected to include a handful of quotes from Persia (modern Iran), as well as notable people and cultures from the Middle East and Arabian Gulf regions.

These quotations have been categorized into six sections, based on my own reflections and professional experiences: Leadership, Coaching and Mentoring, Marketing, Customer Service, Personal Development, and Continuous Learning.

But this is not to say that a quotation found in the Marketing and Customer Service section might not be equally valid to you as a Leadership or Personal Development motivational thought. It all depends on how you reflect on these *Asian Words of Success.*

And that is what I hope you will do as you enjoy this book — and all the other volumes of our *Asian Words of Wisdom* series — reflect upon the words and thoughts of these Asian leaders.

My goal for all the books in our *Asian Words of Wisdom* series is to provide readers with motivational thoughts and quotes that will provide inspiration and motivation for your own growth and development.

After all, as Confucius wrote, *"To be fond of learning is to be near knowledge."*

Steven Howard

August 2016

Asian Words of Success

Foreword

Asia. Largest of the seven continents in the world comprising some 48 countries. Home to roughly 60% of the planet's population, where seven of the world's 10 largest cities (by population) are found.

A land mass so vast that its landscape is wildly varied and it has both the highest (Mount Everest, 8,848m) and the lowest (Dead Sea, -395m) points on Earth. And, as it stands now, nine of the world's ten tallest buildings are in Asia. It is the birthplace of the world's oldest civilizations, biggest religions, and over 2,300 living languages.

Astrology, philosophy, religion, cuisine, spices, silk, fireworks, warfare tactics, tea, yoga, the umbrella, martial arts, the Sony Walkman, noodles and even the much loved Chinos (from the Spanish word for "Chinese") are all Asian contributions to the world. And now Asia is the main driver of global economic growth for the 21st century.

Can anyone really afford to ignore Asia? Can anyone in the West afford not to understand the rich cultural traditions and teachings of this diverse region?

Asian Words of Success

I believe in the power of words. Words can hurt, traumatize, humiliate, belittle, and bring a person to their knees. On the other hand, words can also inspire dreams, lift spirits, stir revolutions, and fill hearts with joy.

When words are not used in the right way, they can bring disharmony and havoc. However, when used right, they can elevate the individual and the world to a higher place of mutual understanding and peace. That is the positive power of words. This is the power that this book possesses.

Within *Asian Words of Success* you will find over 600 motivational quotations and phrases from some of Asia's leading thinkers: Buddha, Confucius, Mahatma Gandhi, Jiddu Krishnamurti, Konosuke Matsushita, Lao-Tzu, Dalai Lama, Sun Tzu, Mother Teresa, and many others.

However, this is not just a book of quotes. This is a book of timeless wisdom — taught, learned, and used throughout history. It is a whole embodiment of timeless principles for one to live by and build a good, successful life.

This book is also filled with inspiration and immensely powerful advice that has stood the test of time. In short, *Asian Words of Success* is the combination of Asia and the power of its written word.

Asian Words of Success

I have known Steven Howard for many years. He has lived the majority of his adult life in Asia (over 21 years), and he has been back to Asia every year since he left. He has traveled to almost all of the Asian countries (in his own words "with the exceptions of Bhutan, Tibet, Nepal, Bangladesh, North Korea, and Brunei") and experienced numerous things that are uniquely Asia.

Most important, Steven has been (and continues to be) a student of Asian wisdom, culture, and history. Throughout his career, Steven has been heavily involved in professional and community organizations, ranging from the American Business Council of Singapore and the Singapore Tourism Promotion Board, to Taekwondo in Australia and President of the International Wine and Food Society of Singapore. His contribution to Asia simply cannot be underestimated or over stated.

Given the Asian mileage he has clocked, meeting locals from so many different countries and so many different cultures, and being involved in so many grassroots activities, it would be fair to say that Steven is more Asian than some Asians themselves.

As the author of over a dozen books, Steven's previous works have consistently been highly praised and reviewed by readers from all over the world. As I am sure this book, and all the others in his *Asian Words of Wisdom* series, will be.

However, the true measure of success is not from these reviews but from how his books touch the professional and personal lives of his readers. I am certain this book will be no different, for it will certainly touch, inspire, and motivate you while you are reading it.

Alex Chan
Singapore
August 2016

Leadership

Most of the literature on leadership we see today comes from Western management and educational thought. The essence of this leadership thinking emphasizes processes, procedures and desired outcomes, with the key skills being:

- Capacity to provide vision

- Ability to identify opportunities

- Big picture perspective and long-term focus

- Ability to plan and manage change

- Emphasis on results and outcomes

- Proficiency in motivating others

- Inspiration

- Confidence

Yet, when we read the words of wisdom from Asia's greatest thinkers and apply these to leadership we see an added focus on communications, people skills, self-awareness, self-understanding, and service.

Merging these two streams of thinking creates the highest levels of leadership practice and implementation.

Additionally, across all cultures there are distinct differences between being a manager and being a leader:

Managers do things right.	Leaders do the right things.
Managers accept the status quo.	Leaders change the status quo.
Managers ensure practice and implementation.	Leaders create and articulate a vision.
Managers focus on the tactical and the short term.	Leaders focus on the strategic and the long term.
Managers tell subordinates what to do and how to do it.	Leaders set a direction, obtain buy-in from others, and allow

	the "how to" to be developed by those handling the implementation.
Managers manage processes, policies, and procedures.	Leaders lead people and people development.
Managers exert command and control over people.	Leaders inspire and motivate people.

In short, managers are planners and controllers, who produce a degree of predictability and order.

Leaders, on the other hand, establish direction, align people, motivate, inspire, and empower others. In addition, leaders must have a belief in themselves and their own capabilities.

The result is that leaders produce change while growing the skills and capabilities of their teams and people.

True leadership requires leaders to share their knowledge, vision, and direction so that others can grow and reach their potential. If everyone in the organization is growing and improving as individuals and as colleagues, then the overall organization will grow, improve and reach its collective potential.

The quotations from Asia's leading thinkers in this chapter were selected to help you develop and increase your own self-confidence and strengthen your own belief in your leadership capabilities.

He who controls others may be powerful but he who has mastered himself is mightier still.

Lao-Tzu

A leader is best when people barely know he exists. Not so good when people obey him and acclaim him. Worse when they despise him. But of a good leader who talks little when his work is done, his aim fulfilled, they will say *"We did it ourselves."*

Lao-Tzu

To lead the people, walk behind them.

Lao-Tzu

If you are a leader, you must have an ideology of leadership. If you lack an ideology, and attempt to decide everything on a case-by-case basis, you will never be capable of strong leadership.

Konosuke Matsushita

The responses of human beings vary greatly under dangerous circumstances. The strong man advances boldly to meet them head on. The weak man grows agitated. But the superior man stands up to fate, endures resolutely in his inner certainty of final success, and bides his time until the onset of reassuring odds.

I Ching

Without knowing the force of words, it is impossible to know men.

Confucius

Inspiration generates inspiration. It gives of itself to whatever it touches.

Paramahansa Yogananda

One who knows much about others may be learned, but one who understands himself is more intelligent. One who controls others may be powerful, but one who has mastered himself is mightier still.

Lao-Tzu

If early death is common in the land, and if death is meted out as punishment, the people do not fear to break the law. To be the executioner in such a land as this, is to be as an unskilled carpenter who cuts his hand when trying to cut wood.

Lao-Tzu

Man becomes the master of difficult situations by refusing the assistance of weak men. He relies on his own strength of character.

I Ching

Those who have knowledge of the natural way do not train themselves in cunning, whilst those who use cunning to rule their lives, and the lives of others, are not knowledgeable of the Tao, nor of natural happiness.

Tao Te Ching

Asian Words of Success

The history of the world is full of men who rose to leadership, by sheer force of self-confidence, bravery, and tenacity.

Mohandas Karamchand (Mahatma) Gandhi

If you must play, decide on three things at the start: the rules of the game, the stakes, and the quitting time.

Chinese Proverb

Thinkers do not accept the inevitable; they turn their efforts toward changing it.

Paramahansa Yogananda

Anything truly revolutionary is created by a few who see what is true and are willing to live according to that truth; but to discover what is true demands freedom from tradition, which means freedom from all fears.

Jiddu Krishnamurti

There are three principles of conduct which the man of high rank should consider specially important: that in his deportment and manner he keep from violence and heedlessness; that in regulating his countenance he keep near to sincerity; and that in his words and tones he keep far from lowness and impropriety.

The Analects

The man who is fond of daring and is dissatisfied with poverty will proceed to insubordination. So will the man who is not virtuous, when you carry your dislike of him to an extreme.

The Analects

A 'No' uttered from deepest conviction is better and greater than a 'Yes' merely uttered to please, or what is worse, to avoid trouble.

Mohandas Karamchand (Mahatma) Gandhi

A journey of a thousand miles must begin with a single step.

Chinese Proverb

Don't be disquieted in time of adversity. Be firm with dignity and self-reliant with vigor.

Chiang Kai-shek

To be conscious of one's own mistakes is the surest way to come out of a difficulty.

Sri Aurobindo

To see what is right and not do it is a lack of courage.

Confucius

Asian Words of Success

I have learned through bitter experience the one supreme lesson to conserve my anger, and as heat conserved is transmitted into energy, even so our anger controlled can be transmitted into a power that can move the world.

Mohandas Karamchand (Mahatma) Gandhi

We must become the change we wish to see in the world.

Mohandas Karamchand (Mahatma) Gandhi

Behave toward everyone as if receiving a great guest.

Confucius

Enthusiasm is the ocean into which we must all take the plunge, waves will be created that will reflect our dynamism.

Swami Chinmayananda Saraswati

The sage does not accumulate (for himself). The more that he expends for others, the more does he possess of his own; the more that he gives to others, the more does he have himself.

Lao-Tzu

If you don't ask, you don't get.

Mohandas Karamchand (Mahatma) Gandhi

Asian Words of Success

Everyone in the world knows that the soft overcomes the hard, and the weak the strong, but no one is able to carry it out in practice.

Lao-Tzu

Vision without action is a daydream. Action with without vision is a nightmare.

Japanese Proverb

To listen well is as powerful a means to influence as to talk well, and is as essential to all true conversations.

Chinese Proverb

The superior man, when he stands alone, is unconcerned, and if he has to renounce the world, he is undaunted.

I Ching

The superior man bends his attention to what is radical. That being established, all practical courses naturally grow up.

Confucius

Those who win every battle are not skillful. Those who render others' armies helpless, without battle, are best of all.

Sun Tzu
The Art of War

Asian Words of Success

The reverse side also has a reverse side.

Japanese Proverb

To know yet to think that one does not know is best.

Tao Te Ching

At the beginning of anything out of the ordinary, the mass of people always dislike it.

Mao Zedong

It's the action, not the fruit of the action, that's important. You have to do the right thing. It may not be in your power, may not be in your time, that there'll be any fruit. But that doesn't mean you stop doing the right thing. You may never know what results come from your action. But if you do nothing, there will be no result.

Mohandas Karamchand (Mahatma) Gandhi

He acts before he speaks, and afterwards speaks according to his actions.

Confucius

If one wants to have an understanding of the matter, look at the North Star by turning towards the south.

Ch'uan-Lao

Given careful attention, any activity may become a window on the universe and a doorway to understanding.

Buddhist Proverb

Monotony is the law of nature. Look at the monotonous manner in which the sun rises. The monotony of necessary occupations is exhilarating and life giving.

Mohandas Karamchand (Mahatma) Gandhi

Adversity is the foundation of virtue.

Japanese Proverb

He will win whose army is animated by the same spirit throughout all its ranks.

Sun Tzu

To know that you do not know is the best. To pretend to know when you do not know is a disease. Only when one recognizes this disease as a disease can one be free from the disease.

Lao-Tzu

There is a magnet in your heart that will attract true friends. That magnet is unselfishness, thinking of others first. When you learn to live for others, they will live for you.

Paramahansa Yogananda

The people may be made to follow a path of action, but they may not be made to understand it.

Confucius

Banish uncertainty. Affirm strength. Hold resolve. Expect Death.

Tao Te Ching

You must not lose faith in humanity. Humanity is an ocean; if a few drops of the ocean are dirty, the ocean does not become dirty.

Mohandas Karamchand (Mahatma) Gandhi

People in their handlings of affairs often fail when they are about to succeed. If one remains as careful at the end as he was at the beginning, there will be no failure.

Lao-Tzu

Yesterday is a dream, tomorrow but a vision. But today well lived makes every yesterday a dream of happiness, and every tomorrow a vision of hope. Look well therefore to this day.

Sanskrit Proverb

You must act as if it is impossible to fail.

Ashanti Proverb

Asian Words of Success

Success often comes to those who dare to act; it seldom goes to the timid who are ever afraid of the consequences.

Jawaharlal Nehru

When you are deluded and full of doubt, even a thousand books of scripture are not enough. When you have realized understanding, even one word is too much.

Fen-Yang

Heroes are made in the hour of defeat. Success is, therefore, well described as a series of glorious defeats.

Mohandas Karamchand (Mahatma) Gandhi

My grandfather once told me: there are two kinds of people, those who do the work and those who take the credit. Try to be in the first group; there is less competition there.

Indira Gandhi

Those who are wise don't consider it a blessing to make no mistakes. They believe instead that the great virtue is the ability to correct mistakes and to continually reinvent oneself.

Wang Yangming

A sly rabbit will have three openings to its den.

Chinese Proverb

Asian Words of Success

In life, it's easy to go along with the flow which eventually leads to being swept away by the tide. If you want to excel, you must show the strength and desire to fight against the tide to achieve what you want.

Wayne Cheng

Satisfaction lies in the effort not the attainment. Full effort is full victory.

Mohandas Karamchand (Mahatma) Gandhi

It takes two hands to clap.

Jiang Zemin

The general who wins the battle makes many calculations in his temple before the battle is fought. The general who loses makes but few calculations beforehand.

Sun Tzu

The foolish reject what they see, not what they think; the wise reject what they think, not what they see.

Huang Po

When the source is deep, the stream is long.

Zen Proverb

Asian Words of Success

Praise shames me, for I secretly beg for it.

Rabindranath Tagore

He who learns but does not think, is lost! He who thinks but does not learn is in great danger!

Confucius

If I keep a green bough in my heart, then the singing bird will come.

Chinese Proverb

One monk shoulders water by himself; two can still share the labor among them. When it comes to three, they have to go thirsty.

Chinese Proverb

There are always ears on the other side of the wall.

Chinese Proverb

Better to light a candle, than to curse the darkness.

Chinese Proverb

Vicious as a tigress can be, she never eats her own cubs.

Chinese Proverb

Asian Words of Success

The person who removes a mountain begins by carrying away small stones.

> Chinese Proverb

There is no one to sweep a common hall.

> Chinese Proverb

It is not the knowing that is difficult, but the doing.

> Chinese Proverb

The wise adapt themselves to circumstances, as water molds itself to the pitcher.

> Chinese Proverb

Virtue never dwells alone; it always has neighbors.

> Chinese Proverb

He who governs by his moral excellence may be compared to the pole star which abides in its place while all other stars bow towards it.

> Chinese Proverb

Men trip not on mountains, they trip on molehills.

> Chinese Proverb

Asian Words of Success

A dog in a kennel barks at his fleas; a dog hunting does not notice them.

Chinese Proverb

I dreamed a thousand new paths. I woke and walked my old one.

Chinese Proverb

Not the cry but the flight of the wild duck leads the flock to fly and follow.

Chinese Proverb

When the work of a great leader is done, and his aim is fulfilled, the people will say *"We did it ourselves."*

Lao-Tzu

The age of people, things, and money is gone. The age of technology, information, and time is here to stay.

Fumiya Tamiaki
President
Molten Corporation

Leading an organization is like frying a small fish. You spoil it with too much poking.

Lao-Tzu

Asian Words of Success

Of the best rulers, the people only know that they exist; the next best they love and praise. The next they fear; and the next they revile. When they do not command the people's faith, some will lose faith in them, and then they resort to oaths! But of the best when their task is accomplished, their work done, the people all remark, "We have done it ourselves."

Lao-Tzu

If we cannot make a profit, that means we are committing a sort of crime against society. We take society's capital, we take their people, we take their materials, yet without a good profit, we are using precious resources that could be better used elsewhere.

Konosuke Matsushita

There is no such thing as a perfect leader either in the past or present, in China or elsewhere. If there is one, he is only pretending, like a pig inserting scallions into its nose in an effort to look like an elephant.

Liu Shaoqi

Follow me if I advance! Kill me if I retreat! Revenge me if I die!

Ngo Dinh Diem

The general who advances without coveting fame and retreats without fearing disgrace, whose only thought is to protect his country and do good service for his sovereign, is the jewel of the kingdom.

Sun Tzu

I am not saying that I enjoy power, but I find it is useful in carrying out the things I want to carry out. If you don't have power and you put out a very reasonable proposal, nobody will implement it. You have to have power. You have to lead. At the same time, you should be sensitive to what your followers think. But if you just respond to the followers and do exactly what they want, then you're not a leader. You have to come out with ideas all the time.

Datuk Seri Dr Mahathir Mohamad
Malaysia Prime Minister

I'm already well into my seventies but no matter how old I get, I intend always to embrace the future. It's the same with a company as with people: turn back and it's all over. You've got to look the future in the eye and step straight ahead.

Eiji Toyoda
Chairman
Toyota

Sincerity is the treasure of a land, for it is in sincerity that the people find their strength in times of hardship.

Confucius

We cannot expect to reach a higher standard of leadership if we do not recognize that meeting our own responsibilities should be a way of life, not a way of gaining rewards.

Mohandas Karamchand (Mahatma) Gandhi

To become an excellent leader, you have to abandon addiction to praise from above and flattery from below. The excellent leader leads least. He studies the distinctive skills and natural inclinations of both those above and those below, and he directs their attention to accomplish what is required to benefit all. When this has been done, all declare they have been part of a worthwhile purpose.

Lao-Tzu

Leaders must have a thorough sense of duty. Leaders must consider their work a mandate from heaven, and they must think that they were born to assume the work. They must live and die for that work, and consider it their one and only mission in life.

Kim Woo-Choong
Korean Entrepreneur

Asian Words of Success

Someone who sees leadership as a means for his own personal gain does not have the credentials to be a leader.

Kim Woo-Choong
Korean Entrepreneur

If we do anything which runs counter to the interests of our people, the result will be a reaction of the people. And that reaction won't be small.

Vo Van Kiet
Vietnam Prime Minister

Our success isn't dependent on proprietary goods and technology, but rather on the experience and motivation of our staff. If I am not successful in tapping the full potential of Mitsui's human assets, then I have failed to fulfill my responsibilities as company president.

Naohiko Kumagai
Chief Executive Officer
Mitsui Group

I have three precious things which I hold fast and prize. The first is gentleness. The second is frugality. The third is humility, which keeps me from putting myself before others. Be gentle and you can be bold. Be frugal and you can be liberal. Avoid putting yourself before others and you can become a leader among men.

Lao-Tzu

Believing that 'human nature is basically good' is a personal philosophy which I apply to Acer. It allows me to establish trust with my staff, my business partners, and my customers.

Stan Shih
Chairman and CEO
ACER Group

We are living in a world about to enter the 21st century, and the bridge beckons. We must cross that bridge with a leader who knows and who thinks. A leader who can be resolute and make the fateful decisions without first consulting one hundred or more economic advisers and counselors.

Philippine Senator Gloria Macapagal Arroyo
(four years before becoming the country's President, 1997)

A leader who allows himself to abuse the power he wields is not thinking of his future good but the immediate gains from corruption.

Datuk Seri Dr Mahathir Mohamad
Malaysia Prime Minister

The ideals of leadership are many. No leader can have all of them. But it suffices if some of these qualities are to be found or are absorbed by a leader.

Datuk Seri Dr Mahathir Mohamad
Malaysia Prime Minister

It is equally important that bad qualities are eschewed by the leader, unconsciously or consciously.

Datuk Seri Dr Mahathir Mohamad
Malaysia Prime Minister

An effective leader is accepted by others. He is someone who would not force his will upon others but would endeavor tactfully to convince others to accept his leadership. At times, a leader must be able to gracefully admit to his mistakes.

Datuk Abdul Khalid Ibrahim
Group Chief Executive
Guthrie

You have to earn the title of leader and you have to dare to take the responsibility. If I have to be tough, I am tough, but with reason to be. I am not tough because I'm the boss.

Sonia Tay
Managing Director
Origins Healthcare

A leader who lacks foresight is not qualified for the position. As a leader, you must keep an eye on the way the times are changing. To find yourself suddenly confronted with a new situation, then to have to search hurriedly for a solution, is no recipe for success.

Konosuke Matsushita

Asian Words of Success

The modern business manager needs to think and act more quickly than his employees. A leader who does not have the sense of responsibility to act in this way should step down at once.

Konosuke Matsushita

A good manager has a vision and sees clearly what's happening and what should be done to adapt quickly to changes and developments. He can grasp the trends that will evolve, and the market place that will emerge. The manager with a vision sees opportunities, while the one with blinkers only bemoans the difficulties. The mark of a good manager is the speed at which he acts on opportunities. The better manager actively shapes the vision and does what needs to be done to realize it.

Rafidah Aziz
Malaysia Minister of International Trade and Industry

Historical insight is the most important foundation for good decision making.

Yasuhiro Nakasone
Japan Prime Minister

Success is more a function of consistent common sense that it is of genius.

Dr. An Wang

A good CEO manages the business well, but an excellent CEO knows how to manage the competition.

Hasan Soedjono
Sempati Air

First they ignore you,

then they laugh at you,

then they fight you,

then you win.

Mohandas Karamchand (Mahatma) Gandhi

When a leader steadily concentrates his people's attention toward a desired destination and then allows them to find their own way to it, they become purposeful and invested. When a leader insists that his own view prevail, his followers waver. When compliance is enforced, followers soon learn evasion and avoidance.

Lao-Tzu

When you create an organization, it soon becomes bureaucratized. So creating means dismantling; you have to repeatedly organize as you dismantle, and dismantle as you build.

Makoto Iida
Chairman and Founder
Secom

Asian Words of Success

You should experience everything for yourself before you say anything about management. It is important to handle what is hardest, what is the most difficult, and learn from your own experiences. There is no substance in just giving superior airs and dashingly signing papers.

Akira Uehara
President
Taisho Pharmaceutical

I believe that the quality of a company is determined by the caliber of its manager. What the manager aspires to, believes in, and dreams of; how he or she lives his or her own life; and, how well his or her employees can relate to these things, determines the caliber of the company.

Takeshi Hayashi
President and CEO
Asahi Solar Corp

I have a kind of hunger that drives me constantly. It is perhaps the same with any successful company. The aspirations of the leader, the intensity of his desire or his sense of crisis tell him whether the status quo should stay or not. I have only one life and I can't help but live it to the full.

Inamori Kazou
Chairman
Kyocera Corporation

Asian Words of Success

When it comes to the relationships among people, you can never build an organization with ideas alone. Even if you do, it will be a weak one. But if you only work with feelings, it will be too sentimental. A true organization is squeezed out from the chaotic intertwining of ideas and feelings. An organization, a company, is never born out of smiles. A company is a product of tears.

Makoto Iida
Chairman and Founder
Secom

What is now required of the leader is "the ability to reform his/her company." It is now not enough to put all efforts in the trade itself. A leader ought to be able to anticipate the changes in times to come and transform the structure of the company itself as well as the current business.

Tetsuo Suzuki
Chairman
Hoya Corporation

If you go through life convinced that your way is always best, all the new ideas in the world will pass you by.

Morita Akio
Chairman
Sony Corporation

Asian Words of Success

I guess that I have excelled only in that I have always tried to go one step ahead of others in doing business. Only a step, or else you would end up being a prophet, far from reality. A merchant is not a prophet.

Kintaro Hattori
Founder
Seiko Corporation

The nobler sort of man emphasizes the good qualities in others, and does not accentuate the bad. The inferior does the reverse.

Confucius

Sometimes it is easier to reduce costs by 30% than by 5%. People tend to think along existing lines when trying to reduce costs by 5%, but they are forced to radically change their ideas when trying to reduce them by 30%, and from this can emerge completely new concepts.

Konosuke Matsushita

If you rest happy and satisfied on your past achievements, the company will become conservative and bureaucratic. Rack your brain, exert yourselves, and each and every one of you should be president of the company.

Koki Ando
Nissin Food Products

Asian Words of Success

If you do not know where you are going, any road will take you there. So you must always know where you want to go and share that destination with your crew. You must provide clear directions how to get there, and organize the optimum mix of resources.

Mohammed Hussein
Managing Director
Aseambankers Malaysia

The corporate environment must promote goal-sharing, unity of purpose, and the sense that everyone from the chief executive to the factory operator is in the same boat. To sail, or sink, as one.

Akio Morita
Chairman
Sony Corporation

Success in any organization is the success in building chemistry between people.

Robert Kwan
Managing Director
McDonald's Singapore

Too many captains will steer the ship up a mountain.

Chinese Proverb

Asian Words of Success

Lead the way, but don't drive all the way. Pause occasionally, check your progress to make sure you have not taken any wrong turns. Nowadays, the corporate roads are so congested it's difficult to make U-turns, and you will lose a lot of ground.

Mohammed Hussein
Managing Director
Aseambankers Malaysia

Person who says it cannot be done should not interrupt person doing it.

Chinese Proverb

Deep doubts, deep wisdom; small doubts, little wisdom.

Chinese Proverb

Perception is strong and sight weak. In strategy it is important to see distant things as if they were close and to take a distanced view of close things.

Miyamoto Musashi

A theory must be tempered with reality.

Jawaharlal Nehru

To chop a tree quickly, spend twice the time sharpening the axe.

Chinese Proverb

Asian Words of Success

All difficult things have their origin in that which is easy, and great things in that which is small.

Lao-Tzu

Dig a well before you are thirsty.

Chinese Proverb

Whatever words we utter should be chosen with care for people will hear them and be influenced by them for good or ill.

Buddha

Those who have high thoughts are ever striving; they are not happy to remain in the same place.

Buddha

The way of a superior man is threefold: Virtuous, he is free from anxieties; Wise, he is free from perplexities; Bold, he is free from fear.

Confucius

We may forget truth for our convenience, but truth does not forget us. Prosperity cannot save itself without moral foundation.

Rabindranath Tagore

Asian Words of Success

A great man is he who has not lost the heart of a child.

Mencius

He who merely knows right principles is not equal to him who loves them.

Confucius

The bamboo that bends is stronger than the oak that resists.

Japanese Proverb

Ask yourself constantly, "What is the right thing to do?"

Confucius

There is in English a very potent word, and you have it in French also, all of the languages of the world have it — it is "No."

Mohandas Karamchand (Mahatma) Gandhi

Strength does not come from physical capacity. It comes from an indomitable will.

Mohandas Karamchand (Mahatma) Gandhi

The superior man thinks always of virtue; the common man thinks of comfort.

Confucius

Asian Words of Success

You must be the change you wish to see.

> Mohandas Karamchand (Mahatma) Gandhi

If there is only a one percent chance of success, a true businessperson sees that one percent as the spark to light a fire.

> Kim Woo-Choong

What the gentleman seeks, he seeks within himself; what the small man seeks, he seeks in others.

> Confucius

Only with a new ruler do you realize the value of the old.

> Burmese Proverb

A true gentleman does not grieve if people do not recognize his merits, yet he grieves at his own want of abilities.

> Confucius

A true gentleman makes demands upon himself but not on others.

> Confucius

To see things in the seed, that is genius.

> Lao-Tzu

Asian Words of Success

By cultivating one's own personal character, he (the ruler) may learn how to govern other people.

Confucius

A dog is not reckoned good because he barks well, and a man is not reckoned wise because he speaks skillfully.

Chuang Tzu

With courage you will dare to take risks, have the strength to be compassionate, and the wisdom to be humble. Courage is the foundation of integrity.

Keshavan Nair

An idea that is developed and put into action is more important than an idea that exists only as an idea.

Buddha

A person who doesn't know, but knows that he doesn't know, is a student; teach him. A person who knows, but doesn't know that he knows, is asleep; awaken him. But a person who knows and knows that he knows is wise; follow him.

Chinese Proverb

Do you hear what the music is saying? "Come follow me and you will find the way. Your mistakes can also lead you to the truth. When you ask, the answer will be given."

Rumi

In one spark of fire there is the whole fire. It can ignite whole cities and nations. One spark. That's how the truth of one person from age to age can shake the whole earth.

Swami Amar Jyoti

Knowing others is intelligence; knowing yourself is true wisdom. Mastering others is strength; mastering yourself is true power.

Lao-Tzu

It is truly said: it does not take much strength to do things, but it requires great strength to decide what to do.

Chow Ching Lie

To hold and fill to overflowing is not as good as to stop in time. Sharpen a knife-edge to its very sharpest, and the edge will not last long.

Lao-Tzu

Asian Words of Success

Many people dream of success. To me, success can only be achieved through repeated failure and introspection.

Soichiro Honda
Founder
Honda Motors

Business, we know, is now so complex and difficult, the survival of firms so hazardous in an environment increasingly unpredictable, competitive, and fraught with danger, that their continued existence depends on the day-to-day mobilization of every ounce of intelligence.

Konosuke Matsushita

Radical change requires adequate authority. A man must have inner strength as well as influential position. What he does must correspond within a higher truth.

Lao-Tzu

If you want something really important to be done you must not merely satisfy the reason, you must move the heart also.

Mohandas Karamchand (Mahatma) Gandhi

In his errors a man is true to type. Observe the errors and you will know the man.

Confucius

Asian Words of Success

A mind all logic is like a knife all blade. It makes the hand bleed that uses it.

Rabindranath Tagore

When eating fruit, think of the person who planted the tree.

Vietnamese Proverb

It is unwise to be too sure of one's own wisdom. It is healthy to be reminded that the strongest might weaken and the wisest might err.

Mohandas Karamchand (Mahatma) Gandhi

The well-run group is not a battlefield of egos.

Lao-Tzu

Coaching and Mentoring

One of the crucial tasks of leaders is to develop the skills and capabilities of their teams and people. This comes from coaching and mentoring them, both individually and collectively.

Every leader should be a coach and mentor to all around them, especially for their direct reports and team members.

This is why every leader should frequently ask themselves two extremely important questions on how they are spending their time:

> *What percentage of your job is focused on getting results, or getting things done?*

> *What percentage of your job is spent on developing people?*

If the answer to the first question is relatively high, such as over 90%, you simply do not have sufficient time to develop your people and your teams.

One of your most important tasks as a leader is to be a mentor. You can only give this task the priority and attention it deserves if you are not spending the large majority of your time focusing on day-to-day results and activities.

A good mentor or coach:

- Builds self-respect in subordinates and colleagues
- Shows respect to all
- Lives and breathes integrity
- Is fair (and is seen to be fair)
- Values and reinforces the ideas of others
- Provides both immediate and on-going feedback
- Reinforces the right things

Helping people feel good about their efforts, as well as their accomplishments, is one of the secrets to good mentoring and coaching.

The word **jingshen** in the Chinese language means *spirit and vivacity*. This is a word that leaders (being coaches and mentors) should take to heart, because the combination of spirit and vivacity can propel individuals and organizations to heights previously unscaled.

We all know that the best team does not win every sporting contest. A good coach can inspire his or her players to outperform another team comprising better players and greater raw talent.

The same is true in the business world. A good leader, who by definition is also a good mentor and coach, can create a spirit of unity, togetherness, and purpose that energizes and invigorates a working unit (or an entire organization) to overcome internal hurdles or to outperform a competitor with deeper pockets and greater resources.

As noted above, helping people feel good about their efforts and accomplishments is a secret to effective leadership. This skill separates the powerful, inspirational, good bosses from the dictatorial, demanding, not respected ones.

The quotations in this section will help you become the kind of highly effective leader you desire to be.

Tell me and I'll forget, show me and I may remember, involve me and I'll understand.

Chinese Proverb

Asian Words of Success

One kind word can warm three winter months.

Japanese Proverb

It is not a question of managing by technical supremacy, or ensuring that I know my subject ten times more that those who work for me. It's a matter of being their coach and mentor and providing them the latitude to grow.

Peter Lau
Chairman and CEO
Giordano International

When one gives whatever one can without restraint, the barriers of individuality break down. It no longer becomes possible to tell whether it is the student offering himself to the teacher, or the teacher offering herself to the student. One sees only two immaculate beings, reflecting one another like a pair of brilliant mirrors.

Lao-Tzu

When you praise somebody, what matters most is that you genuinely appreciate him or her. If you think that person means nothing to you, holds no expectation or worth for you, any words of praise you might contrive out of a sense of duty will accomplish nothing.

Konosuke Matsushita
Founder
Matsushita Electric Industrial

Asian Words of Success

Deal with the faults of others as gently as with your own.

Chinese Proverb

Kindness in words creates confidence. Kindness in thinking creates profoundness. Kindness in giving creates love.

Lao-Tzu

Virtues are acquired through endeavor, which rests wholly upon yourself. So, to praise others for their virtues can but encourage one's own efforts.

Nagarjuna

Desire excites. Excitement may sometimes elevate us but will depress us eventually. Inspiration elevates further and further.

Swami Amar Jyoti

Giving vision to his staff and helping them achieve it is what leadership is all about. The time of having one hero in the company is over. The role of leadership today is to form a cooperative tie that binds employees.

Bae Soon Hoon
CEO
Daewoo Electronics

To gain complete trust from someone is to obtain an invitation into their soul.

Wayne Cheng

If troops are punished before they have grown loyal, they will be disobedient. If not obedient, it is difficult to employ them. But if troops have become loyal, but discipline is not enforced, the general can't employ them either.

Sun Tzu

It is not for the system to dictate the moves of people, but for people to dictate the system. A company where the system moves its people will lose its vigor and will decline. It is the company where people move the system that develops and grows.

Gaishi Hiraiwa
Chairman and CEO
Tokyo Electric Power

Before you speak, let your words pass through three gates. At the first ask, "Is it true?" At the second ask, "Is it necessary?" At the third ask, "Is it kind?"

Sufi Proverb

Asian Words of Success

Our motto is "train the people, organize the people, motivate the people."

Fang Hong
Senior Engineer and Managing Director
Shanghai Volkswagen Automotive Co. Ltd

The gem cannot be polished without friction, nor man perfected without trial.

Confucius

Give a man a fish and you feed him for a day. Teach him how to fish and you feed him for a lifetime.

Lao-Tzu

Patience is power; with time and patience the mulberry leaf becomes silk.

Chinese Proverb

He whose army is animated by the same spirit throughout all the ranks will win.

Sun Tzu

Whenever you have truth it must be given with love, or the message and the messenger will be rejected.

Mohandas Karamchand (Mahatma) Gandhi

Asian Words of Success

Without too much trouble, people can keep to the main road. But people love to be distracted, and perspective is difficult.

Tao Te Ching

Pay heed to nourishing the troops. Do not unnecessarily fatigue them. Unite them in spirit.

Sun Tzu

One cannot live in this world without the support of others.

Okinawan Proverb

A true gentleman always points out the goodness in others but does not speak loudly of their faults.

Confucius

The way to change others' minds is with affection, not anger.

The Dalai Lama

Life's errors cry for the merciful beauty that can modulate their isolation into a harmony with the whole.

Rabindranath Tagore

Speak or act with a pure mind and happiness will follow you as your shadow, unshakable.

The Dhammapada

Men's natures are alike – it is their habits that carry them far apart.

Confucius

We treat employees as a member of the family. If management takes the risk of hiring them, we have to take responsibility for them.

Akio Morita

There should be less talk; a preaching point is not a meeting point. What do you do then? Take a broom and clean someone's house. That says enough.

Mother Teresa

No one ever won a chess game by betting on each move. Sometimes you have to move backward to get a step forward.

Amar Gopal Bose

There is an English proverb that says "there are no bad students, only bad teachers." I believe it also applies to a company. There are no bad employees, only bad managers.

T. S. Lin
Tatung Co.

Praise out of season, or tactlessly bestowed, can freeze the heart as much as blame.

Pearl S. Buck

Kind words can be short and easy to speak, but their echoes are truly endless.

Mother Teresa

Focus on both people and the results. Without people a leader cannot get results. Without results you will get nowhere.

Jayakar Rangarajan
CEO
Syntel India

Marketing and Business Success

Markets continue to change at an accelerating rate. Industry boundaries are constantly blurring. Customer needs are more specific and individualized than ever before.

The forces reshaping the world economy today are more numerous, more interwoven, and combine to be more powerful than any other combination of economic and political change since the Industrial Revolution.

In fact, change is happening so rapidly that the countless reorganizations, mergers, spin-offs, restructurings, downsizings, break-ups and new business start-ups make the business community almost seem out of control.

Meanwhile, customers continue to present a vast array of challenges and opportunities. Unfortunately, these challenges and opportunities are unlikely to be as apparent as in the past or as easy to grasp.

Just think about all the choices and options available to customers today. Rare is the organization that finds itself without numerous competitors. Even rarer is the customer without a range of options, choices, or substitute products for the solutions he or she seeks.

The best way to take care of your prospects and customers is to tailor or customize your products and service offerings as much as you profitably can. Treat your customers as individuals — with individual wants, needs, desires, likes and dislikes — at all customer touch points and you will be well on your way to developing customer loyalty.

Two of the three ways to grow any business (getting your customers to buy in larger volumes or more frequently) requires concentrating on your current customer base. For many businesses, the third way (increasing the number of customers) also requires a focus on the current customer base since a large percentage of new customers is often generated though referrals and social media comments made by your current customers.

This means having a dedicated effort to focus on your current customers, particularly your key customers, is more important than ever.

Keeping customers loyal is an art form, not a science. As is true of all good marketing practices.

Marketing is, after all, an art; not a scientific discipline.

Asian Words of Success

My own personal marketing philosophy is very simple: ***if it touches the customer, it's a marketing issue.***™

The corollary to this is another of my deep-seated marketing beliefs: *if you don't take care of your customers, someone else will.*

Those are my views. Let's see how we can apply the thoughts of Asia's leading thinkers to the art of marketing.

We can't simply rely on a long-established reputation. We have to offer exactly what our customers require, even if we have to give up some.

Ichiro Inumaru
President
Imperial Hotel

The reputation of a thousand years may be determined by the conduct of one hour.

Japanese Proverb

A wise hawk hides its claws.

Japanese Proverb

Customers' voices are more precious than any other management guidebooks.

> Naomi Munetsugu
> President
> Ichibanya

If you know the enemy and know yourself, you need not fear a hundred battles.

> Sun Tzu

I have always believed that the company name is the life of an enterprise. It carries responsibility and guarantees the quality of the product.

> Akio Morita

Divisions are imaginary lines drawn by small minds.

> Paramahansa Yogananda

Study the past, if you would divine the future.

> Confucius

If names are not correct, language is not in accordance with the truth of things. If language is not in accordance with the truth of things, affairs cannot be carried on to success.

> Confucius

Asian Words of Success

Clay is molded to make a vessel, but the utility of the vessel lies in the space where there is nothing. Thus, taking advantage of what is, we recognize the utility of what is not.

Lao-Tzu

In an archery contest, when the stakes are earthenware tiles a contestant shoots with skill. When the stakes are belt buckles he becomes hesitant, and if the stakes are pure gold he becomes nervous and confused. There is no difference as to his skill but, because there is something he prizes, he allows outward considerations to weigh on his mind. All those who consider external things important are stupid within.

Chuang Tzu

With time and patience the mulberry leaf becomes a silk gown.

Chinese Proverb

Add legs to the snake after you have finished drawing it.

Chinese Proverb

The customer no longer knows what is possible.

Akio Morita

Asian Words of Success

Crows everywhere are equally black.

Chinese Proverb

Dream different dreams while on the same bed.

Chinese Proverb

No wind, no waves.

Chinese Proverb

Of all the stratagems, to know when to quit is the best.

Chinese Proverb

Only the man who crosses the river at night knows the value of the light of day.

Chinese Proverb

Paper can't wrap up a fire.

Chinese Proverb

We are not so much concerned if you are slow as when you come to a halt.

Chinese Proverb

A weasel comes to say "Happy New Year" to the chickens.

Chinese Proverb

Without rice, even the cleverest housewife cannot cook.

Chinese Proverb

There are many paths to the top of the mountain, but the view is always the same.

Chinese Proverb

The lesson is that consumers everywhere will not accept anything less than the best. Even countries previously dismissed as being less developed are fast changing from sellers' to buyers' markets. Given this scenario, the only way for companies to compete is to meet world-class quality standards.

Richard Hu
Singapore Finance Minister

The more you sweat in Peacetime, the less you bleed during War.

Chinese Proverb

Pure gold does not fear furnace.

Chinese Proverb

He who rides the tiger can never dismount.

Chinese Proverb

The 21st century will be one during which an enterprise's fate will be largely determined by the quality of its products. Only by continuously improving quality and efficiency can an enterprise survive the tough market competition.

> Ding Qidong
> Chief Engineer
> China State Bureau of Technical Supervision

We can no longer compete on low cost. Competition must now be based on capabilities.

> Tan Chin Nam
> Managing Director
> Singapore Economic Development Board

No matter how much advertising you do, if the product in question is not of good quality, it will never sell. You will lack confidence when advertising, and, what's more, once the consumers decide that there is no truth in the advertisement, that's it. What comes first and foremost is to make quality products.

> Shinjiro Torii
> Founder
> Suntory Ltd

He whose ranks are united in purpose will be victorious!

> Sun Tzu

Asian Words of Success

If we merely try to be excellent, our gap with the world's top companies will remain because they keep improving. Only by seeking super-excellence can we reach their level or overtake them.

Chay Tae-won
Chairman
Sunkyong Group

It is the quality of our work that will please God and not the quantity.

Mohandas Karamchand (Mahatma) Gandhi

Don't sell customers goods that they are attracted to. Sell them goods that will benefit them.

Konosuke Matsushita

Taking a step....is always better than not taking a step.

M H Jou
Vice President
China Maritime Transport

Often, highly successful new products do not necessarily represent a new breakthrough in technology, but just a more creative and innovative application of existing know-how.

Yeo Cheow Tong
Singapore Trade and Industry Minister

Bear in mind that an unpolished plan which is vigorously executed will be more successful than a perfect plan that takes longer to produce and is implemented with less determination. It is often better to decide the main thrust of the attack, strike energetically, gain experience, learn what works and what does not, then reassess the new situation, devise fresh plans, and take another step. If one spends too long preparing elaborate plans, one will lose not only time, but also initiative.

Lee Hsien Loong
Singapore Deputy Prime Minister

An organization will not endure for the long term when its leaders depend on aggression as a constant strategy. Aggression has consequences — even when it is successful it breeds enemies. Weak enemies may combine and become strong.

Lao-Tzu

The world is changing, it is important for a manager to thoroughly pursue the reason for the change and see the situation objectively. You should never ever make a judgment based only on your own past experiences.

Toshifumi Suzuki
President and CEO
Ito-Yokado Group

Management consists of "constancy" and "change." Offering good quality products at low prices is the "constancy" side of the principle, while striving for new product development and business is the "change" aspect.

Shonosuke Kuroda
Chairman
Kokuyo Co

Take the noodle vendor, who is always trying to make the best possible tasting soup for his customers. Because the noodle vendor is always thinking about how to make the best soup, he will play with his recipes, listen to his customers, always change. He has an unshackled mind.

Masaharu Matsushita
Chairman
Panasonic

When you develop products, first and foremost, you must always think of what kind of products can make many people happy. In other words, before thinking of what can sell or what can be profitable, you must think of the contribution you can make to society.

Tadao Kashio
Founder
Casio Computer Company

Asian Words of Success

For Mitsubishi Corporation, change is much more that a buzzword: it is crucial to our profitability and growth. The truism that change occurs daily means that businesses must adjust their strategies and practices in accordance to such changes in the operating environment. To be a market leader, it is not sufficient simply to react; a business must anticipate emerging trends and move proactively to profit from them.

Minoru Makihara
President and CEO
Mitsubishi Corporation

If what you are going to do is based on what is already known, you cannot expect innovation.

Masaru Ibuku
Co-Founder
Sony

To advance our cause to the 21st century in an all-round way requires us to seize opportunities without fail, and blaze new trails instead of following the beaten tracks.

Jiang Zemin
Chinese Communist Party Leader

Just as a picture is drawn by an artist, surroundings are created by the activities of the mind.

Buddha

Asian Words of Success

We are faced with intense competition for market share. What must we do to win this battle for markets? We need to create an innovative edge in marketing in order to successfully market and reach our target markets, especially the exploding Asian middle class segment. An innovative marketing edge can only be built on the foundation of a corporate culture that drives an organization to adapt rapidly and continuously in order to fit into the 21st century environment. Companies need to make a paradigm shift and recognize that rapid and continuous change has become an essential component of the daily operations of a company in striving to expand and sustain market share.

Tan Sri Dato Dr Loy Hean Heong
President and Chief Executive
MBf Group of Companies

The biggest mistake anyone can make is to focus on the competitor. You focus on the consumer and you will get it right.

Keki Dadiseth
Chairman
Hindustan Lever

Pick a battle you can win and win it convincingly.

Mao Zedong

Asian Words of Success

Too few managers consciously try to set plans and build organizations as if they see all key customers equidistant from the corporate center. The word "overseas" has no place in Honda's vocabulary because it sees itself as equidistant from all key customers.

Kenichi Ohmae

Customer satisfaction is an essential, but invisible, feature of any successful product.

Takashi (Tachi) Kiuchi
Chairman & CEO
Matsushita Electric America

People are living things, with emotions and sensitivity. Can everything be reduced to simply ones and zeroes? There is still something to be said for maintaining 'analog' relationships with customers that allow us to better understand their different needs.

Masaharu Matsushita
Chairman
Panasonic

When an elephant is in trouble even a frog will kick him.

Hindu Proverb

Happiness is the absence of the striving for happiness.

Chuang Tzu

Asian Words of Success

The business world is a jungle in which laws are set by customers. Companies — the prey — are all subject to its changing laws. In the merciless animal kingdom, as in business, doing things right the first time is a matter of survival.

Rene T Domingo
Sime Darby Professor of Manufacturing
Asian Institute of Management

As we enter the Era of Choices, there is no guarantee that satisfied customers will become loyal customers. Satisfaction has increasingly become a commodity. It is only the process, not the end result. The final goal of The Marketing Company is customer loyalty. Customer loyalty has become the moving target every Marketing Company must pursue to remain competitive. What matters most to The Marketing Company now is the quality of profit, not just the quantity of profit. It is already evident that customer attraction activities cost a company much more than a customer retention program; the cost to acquire a new customer will cost more than retaining one good customer. Profits, therefore, should come from old, existing customers rather than from new, first-time buyers.

Hermawan Kartajaya
President
Indonesia Marketing Association

Asian Words of Success

Opportunities multiply as they are seized.

Sun Tzu

Climb mountains to see lowlands.

Chinese Proverb

Talk doesn't cook rice.

Chinese Proverb

When you want to test the depths of a stream, don't use both feet.

Chinese Proverb

Goodness speaks in a whisper, evil shouts.

Tibetan Proverb

Deceive the rich and powerful if you will, but don't insult them.

Japanese Proverb

The go-between wears out a thousand sandals.

Japanese Proverb

The top of the hill is but the bottom of another mountain.

Ankit Jamwal

Be not afraid of going slowly. Be afraid of standing still.

Chinese Proverb

As circumstances are favorable, one should modify one's plans.

Sun Tzu

A clever fighter is one who not only wins, but excels in winning with ease.

Sun Tzu

Do not repeat the tactics which have gained you one victory but let your methods be regulated by the infinite variety of circumstances.

Sun Tzu

Patience is the key to contentment.

Prophet Muhammad

Problems are sent to us as gifts.

Chinese Proverb

Better to do a good deed near at home than to go far away to burn incense.

Chinese Proverb

When strength is expended, and resources consumed, even wise generals cannot achieve a good result.

> Sun Tzu

The journey of a thousand miles begins with a single step.

> Chinese Proverb

Be extremely subtle, to the point of formlessness. Be extremely mysterious, to the point of soundlessness. Thereby you can be the director of the opponent's fate.

> Sun Tzu

They conquer by strategy.

> Sun Tzu

Invincibility lies in the defense; the possibility of victory in the attack.

> Sun Tzu

Weigh the situation, then move.

> Sun Tzu

Ground which both we and the enemy can traverse with equal ease is called accessible.

> Sun Tzu

If one gains the advantage of the ground then even weak and soft troops can conquer the enemy.

Sun Tzu

Fight downhill — do not ascend to attack.

Sun Tzu

Generally, in battle, use the normal force to engage; use the extraordinary to win.

Sun Tzu

In general, occupy a position which facilitates your action.

Sun Tzu

In enclosed ground, resourcefulness is required.

Sun Tzu

Prepare ambushes, seize opportunities.

Sun Tzu

Encamp on high ground facing the sunny side!

Sun Tzu

In planning, never a useless move; in strategy no step taken in vain.

Sun Tzu

Asian Words of Success

Anciently the skillful warriors first made themselves invincible and awaited the enemy's moment of vulnerability.

Sun Tzu

Speed is the essence of war.

Sun Tzu

If you are able to hold critical points on his strategic roads the enemy cannot come.

Sun Tzu

It is sufficient to estimate the enemy situation correctly and to concentrate your strength to capture him.

Sun Tzu

Never rely on the glory of the morning or the smiles of your mother-in-law.

Japanese Proverb

If you want to attain something, you should get right about working on it.

Zen Master Dōgen

The fruit drops when it is ripe.

Zen Proverb

Asian Words of Success

People in their handlings of affairs often fail when they are about to succeed. If one remains as careful at the end as he was at the beginning, there will be no failure.

Lao-Tzu

The season of failure is the best time for sowing the seeds of success.

Paramahansa Yogananda

The wise boldly pick up a truth as soon as they hear it. Don't wait for a moment, or you'll lose your head.

Hsueh-Dou

Sometimes it is more important to discover what one cannot do, than what one can do.

Lin Yutang

Use a mirror in difficult times. You will see both the cause and resolution.

Tao Te Ching

Plan the whole year in the spring.

Chinese Proverb

People naturally fear misfortune and long for good fortune, but if the distinction is carefully studied, misfortune often turns out to be good fortune and good fortune to be misfortune. The wise man learns to meet the changing circumstances of life with an equitable spirit, being neither elated by success nor depressed by failure.

Buddha

Whatever is flexible and flowing will tend to grow. Whatever is rigid and blocked will wither and die.

Tao Te Ching

At the outset, the man does not comprehend the nature of prevailing forces nor does he perceive them as a connected whole. This superficial view is acceptable for the masses, but the superior man should know better.

I Ching

The art of life is a constant readjustment to our surroundings.

Kakuzo Okakura

It does not matter how slowly you go so long as you do not stop.

Confucius

Asian Words of Success

When the character of a man is not clear to you, look at his friends.

Japanese Proverb

The future depends on what we do in the present.

Mohandas Karamchand (Mahatma) Gandhi

Customer Service

Excellent customer service is driven by customer satisfaction; resulting in a strategic advantage for your organization — with a direct impact on repeat business, customer recommendations to others, market share, revenue, and profit.

To deliver excellent customer satisfaction, your organization must have a full understanding of the wants, needs, desires, likes, and dislikes of your customers and prospects. I would also suggest you need to have an organization-wide attitude that understands a person or organization is not truly your customer until *the second time they buy.*

That's right. I recommend you do not consider anyone a customer until the second time they buy from you. The first time they buy they are merely a trial user. Unless they achieve satisfaction from the purchase and use of your products or services, they may be unlikely to repeat their business with you.

Hence, taking care of the customer goes beyond the mere sales cycle and includes all post-purchase activities such as use, repair, servicing, customer service, warranties, trade-in, or re-sale.

Service-successful companies build employee customer service professionalism in their employees via several well-established processes and methodologies. They establish personal accountability of individual employees. They ensure staff understand how their jobs fit into the entire organization. They create multifunctional service teams. They open multiple communications channels with their staff and use these rigorously. They reward extraordinary service actions.

Successful service-oriented companies also explain to staff the importance of customer service, the need for problem-free service, and the benefits to the organization (and themselves) of delivering excellent service to customers.

None of the tactics used by service excellent companies is necessarily revolutionary. What is most outstanding is how energetically and comprehensively these companies work at creating, executing, and constantly improving their customer service programs.

Underlining all these imperatives is a simple belief: customer relations mirror employee relations. The greater employee engagement and satisfaction, the greater the customer experience will be.

Likewise, employees must first perceive and understand within their own organizations whatever it is management wants customers to perceive. This operates most directly with customer contact employees, the pivotal people in any service business. They internalize messages passed within their organization, and in turn broadcast these messages to customers.

In a study of bank branch employees and their customers, a researcher confirmed this relationship. When employees reported that their branch emphasized service, customers also reported superior banking experiences and were more highly satisfied.

The quotations and excerpts in this section have been chosen to help you reflect on the true nature of the customer service professionalism in your organization and the steps you can take to consistently deliver high-quality customer service.

After-sales service is more important than assistance before sales. It is through such service that one gets permanent customers.

Konosuke Matsushita

Wait on the customer rather than await the customer.

N.U. Jayawardena
Founder
Sampath Bank

You cannot shake hands with a clenched fist.

Indira Mohandas Karamchand (Mahatma) Gandhi

A customer is the most important visitor on our premises. He is not dependent on us. We are dependent on him. He is not an interruption in our work. He is the purpose of it. He is not an outsider in our business. He is part of it. We are not doing him a favor by serving him. He is doing us a favor by giving us an opportunity to do so.

Mohandas Karamchand (Mahatma) Gandhi

We consistently seek out very demanding customers, which challenges us to perform even better.

Suresh
Managing Director
Sundram Fasteners

Quality people are the company's most important resource and the most rigorous quality control process we apply is for staff selection.

> Dr. Cheong Choong Kong
> Deputy Chairman and Chief Executive Officer
> Singapore Airlines

The unremitting forces of competition compel us sometimes to introduce novelties into the aircraft cabin, over and above what we would normally provide for our distinctive quality of service. What counts in the end is the human dimension of our service, not just gizmos. That is where careful recruitment, rigorous training, and superior leadership are decisive. Our staff make that vital difference.

> Mr. J Y Pillay
> Chairman
> Singapore Airlines

Customer satisfaction begins with a reliable, quality product designed to meet the needs of its end users. The customer must feel proud of their purchase and gratified with the service they received, if assistance is necessary.

> Albert Kim
> President
> Samsung Electronics

Customers are jade; merchandise is grass.

> Chinese Proverb

Today, quality work is 90 per cent attitude and 10 per cent knowledge.

Patrick Sung
IBM China-Hongkong Corp

In case of rain, protect your customers with your umbrellas and walk them to their cars.

Toyota Sales Manual

One hundred minus one can't be 99 in the hotel business — it may be zero. If one employee out of hundreds gives a bad impression to a certain customer, it will be 100% damage for our hotel image for that customer.

Ichiro Inumaru
President
Imperial Hotel

I consider each customer as a family member who deserves nothing but the best service.

Tammy Toh
Shop Manager
Giordano Singapore

Technology is really not a competitive advantage anymore: it is customer service.

Allen Yeung
Area Head of Personnel
Standard Chartered Bank

Our job is not just to fly people from A to B, but to have them enjoy the flight. We're not in the transportation business, we're in the service business. All airlines claim this, but the big difference is not the objectives set out by management, or in the ads developed by the marketing department, it is in the delivery of service.

Michael Tan
Deputy Managing Director (Commercial)
Singapore Airlines

The BEST customer is the one that complains. "Nice" customers just go away without telling you. Approximately 96 percent of unhappy customers are silent customers. But they cost you millions.

Dr. Chang Yu Sang
Director of the Asian Management Center
Boston University

The fundamental cause of poor quality is that we no longer act according to Matsushita's basic policies. If quality is bad and a product does not sell well, we have to stop the factory and improve the product. When we make goods of inferior quality, we are not contributing to society, and that is inconsistent with our basic policies.

Konosuke Matsushita

In the past, government officials treated people differently than the private sector did. To the private sector, people are customers who bring profit to the company, while people are nobody to public officials. So the important thing is to change the thinking. Government offices should use some private sector techniques by realizing that their future depends on the customer's satisfaction.

Mrs. Dhipavadee Meksawan
Deputy General
Thailand Office of the Civil Service Commission

Being sincere and honest, my father treats his customers like friends. He tells his customers frankly what is the right choice for them rather than trying to make the most profit out of them.

Supon Pornnirunlit

Straightforwardness, without the rules of propriety, becomes rudeness.

Confucius

The highest form of human intelligence is to observe yourself without judgment.

Jiddu Krishnamurti

Asian Words of Success

He who smiles rather than rages is always the stronger.

Japanese Proverb

It is not the failure of others to appreciate your abilities that should trouble you, but rather your failure to appreciate theirs.

Confucius

The policy of being too cautious is the greatest risk of all.

Jawaharlal Nehru

Our prime purpose in this life is to help others. And if you can't help them, at least don't hurt them.

The Dalai Lama

There is a Proverb in the USA that the customer is king. But in Japan, the customer is GOD.

Tak Kimoto
Sumitronics

Perfect kindness acts without thinking of kindness.

Lao-Tzu

For every hundred men hacking away at the branches of a diseased tree, only one will stoop to inspect the roots.

Chinese Proverb

Asian Words of Success

Know well what leads you forward and what holds you back, and choose the path that leads to wisdom.

Buddha

The person who removes a mountain begins by carrying away small stones.

Chinese Proverb

The higher type of man clings to virtue, the lower type of man clings to material comfort. The higher type of man cherishes justice, the lower type of man cherishes the hope of favors to be received.

Confucius

Better service for the customer is for the good of the public, and this is the true purpose of enterprise.

Konosuke Matsushita

The expectations of life depend upon diligence; the mechanic that would perfect his work must first sharpen his tools.

Confucius

Don't let a little dispute injure a great friendship.

Dalai Lama

Personal Development

Today, the path to personal self-realization and personal growth might traverse a combination of spiritual reading, yoga, meditation, essential oils, time spent in quiet nature settings, aromatherapy, or homeopathic healing techniques.

Whatever the path chosen by the individual, it is clear that a key concern in today's world is the on-going need and desire for personal development and the integration of many, and perhaps all, aspects of one's human and spiritual being.

In the business world, the need for personal and professional development has never been greater. The skills needed for career success and advancement are changing rapidly, and no longer include only the technical skills required to perform tasks. Many so-called "soft" skills such as influence, leading others, working in teams, cross-border communications, cultural diversity, developing others, and conflict management are all required for success in today's workplace.

Additionally, today's workers need to hone their skills in the areas of self-awareness, self-confidence, trustworthiness, organizational awareness, market awareness, and achievement orientation.

Thus, the need for self-development is evident on both a personal and a workplace level.

Additionally, much is written these days about the need for greater balance in one's life, especially around the work vs. life balance equilibrium.

The stresses and demands of modern-day living are leaving many with the feeling that their lives are out of balance. Many people struggle to cope with the day-to-day juggling of careers, families, child rearing, personal interests, and social commitments.

The deep-seated need for balance in our lives, and in our bodies, is depicted through the yin and yang concepts that form a foundation for many personal belief systems in Asia. Not surprisingly, Asia's leading thinkers have historically been a valued resource for insights into self-awareness and personal development.

For instance, the words of Confucius have long represented a more reflective and deliberate approach to life than normally found in today's fast-paced and hectic age. With a focus on social harmony, self-improvement, and firm ethical principles, the words and writings of Confucius are a wealth of guidance on topics such as the development of personal virtue, the importance of the family, and the need for continuous cultivation of knowledge.

As in days of Confucius, what is truly needed today is a focus on personal development that is for the good of society and the community, not just for the betterment of one's self. This is best expressed in the Japanese word **kyosei**, which essentially means *living and working together for the common good.*

May the passages found in this section be a source of light and inspiration for all readers, and help you bring **kyosei** into your lives, workplaces and communities.

Learn to be calm and you will always be happy.

Paramahansa Yogananda

It is better to conquer yourself than to win a thousand battles.

Buddha

When you look for truth outside yourself, it gets farther away.

Dongshan Liangjie

He who asks is a fool for five minutes, but he who does not ask remains a fool forever.

Chinese Proverb

You indulge in Self Improvement and all you have to show for it is an improved self.

Ram Tzu

If you want to know your past, look into your present conditions. If you want to know your future, look into your present actions.

Buddhist Proverb

It is not enough to work conscientiously. No matter what kind of job you have, you should think of yourself as being completely in charge of and responsible for your work, like being the president of your own company. By doing so, not only can appropriate devices be made and new discoveries born, you will also greatly assist your own self-development.

Konosuke Matsushita

Increase of material comforts, it may be generally laid down, does not in any way whatsoever conduce to moral growth.

Mohandas Karamchand (Mahatma) Gandhi

If your mental attitude changes constantly under the pressure of tests, you are losing the battle of life. He who is undefeated within is a truly victorious person.

Paramahansa Yogananda

Those who, relying upon themselves only, not looking for assistance from anyone besides themselves, it is they who will reach the top-most height.

Buddha

You must find the place inside yourself where nothing is impossible.

Deepak Chopra

Yesterday I was clever, so I wanted to change the world. Today I am wise, so I am changing myself.

Rumi

To make the right choices in life, you have to get in touch with your soul. To do this, you need to experience solitude, which most people are afraid of, because in the silence you hear the truth and know the solutions.

Deepak Chopra

Every moment I shape my destiny with a chisel I am a carpenter of my own soul.

Rumi

Think lightly of yourself and think deeply of the world.
Miyamoto Musashi

The great battle of meditation is with restless thoughts.
Paramahansa Yogananda

In the battle of life one has to learn to be a hero. Heroism is not egoism. It is an expression of the native dignity of the ego wedded to the infinite.
Paramahansa Yogananda

You have to grow from the inside out. None can teach you, none can make you spiritual. There is no other teacher but your own soul.
Swami Vivekananda

Strength does not come from physical capacity. It comes from an indomitable will.
Mohandas Karamchand (Mahatma) Gandhi

You seek too much information and not enough transformation.
Sai Baba

Smiling away your troubles requires a clear conscience that harbors no insincerity.
Paramahansa Yogananda

Because you don't analyze yourself, you remain always psychological furniture, never changing.

Paramahansa Yogananda

Holding on to anger is like grasping a hot coal with the intent of throwing it at someone else; you are the one who gets burned.

Buddha

There is nothing more yielding than water, yet when acting on the solid and strong, its gentleness and fluidity have no equal in anything. The weak can overcome the strong, and the supple overcome the hard. Although this is known far and wide, few put it into practice in their lives.

Lao-Tzu

Being deeply loved by someone gives you strength, while loving someone deeply gives you courage.

Lao-Tzu

Tao points out, "The snow goose need not bathe to make itself white." Neither need you do anything but be yourself. If a man does only what is required of him, he is a slave. If a man does more than is required of him, he is a free man.

Chinese Proverb

Asian Words of Success

Do not overrate what you have received, nor envy others. He who envies others does not obtain peace of mind.

Buddha

Life is like a game of cards. The hand that is dealt you represents determinism; the way you play it is free will.

Jawaharlal Nehru

Ambition never comes to an end.

Yoshida Kenko

By three methods we may learn wisdom: First, by reflection, which is noblest; Second, by imitation, which is easiest; and third by experience, which is the bitterest.

Confucius

The perfecting of one's self is the fundamental base of all progress and all moral development.

Confucius

Peace comes from within. Do not seek it without.

Buddha

When drinking water remember the source.

Chinese Proverb

He who sacrifices his conscience to ambition burns a picture to obtain the ashes.

Chinese Proverb

Utopia must spring in the private bosom before it can flower in civic virtue, inner reforms leading naturally to outer ones. A man who has reformed himself will reform thousands.

Paramahansa Yogananda

A course sieve catches little. A fine mesh catches more. If you want the subtle, be refined, But prepare to deal with the coarse.

Tao Te Ching

If you want to awaken all of humanity, then awaken all of yourself, if you want to eliminate the suffering in the world, then eliminate all that is dark and negative in yourself. Truly, the greatest gift you have to give is that of your own self-transformation.

Lao-Tzu

Without an acquaintance with the rules of propriety, it is impossible for the character to be established.

Confucius

Love thy neighbor as thyself: Do not to others what thou wouldst not wish be done to thyself. Forgive injuries. Forgive thy enemy, be reconciled to him, give him assistance, invoke [the Principle] in his behalf.

Confucius

Respectfulness, without the rules of propriety, becomes laborious bustle; carefulness, without the rules of propriety, becomes timidity; boldness, without the rules of propriety, becomes insubordination; straightforwardness, without the rules of propriety, becomes rudeness.

Confucius

Warm weather fosters growth: cold weather destroys it. Thus a man with an unsympathetic temperament has a scant joy: but a man with a warm and friendly heart overflowing blessings, and his beneficence will extend to posterity.

Hung Tzu-Cheng

There is more to life than increasing its speed.

Mohandas Karamchand (Mahatma) Gandhi

Although gold dust is precious, when it gets in your eyes it obstructs vision.

Hsi-Tang

Asian Words of Success

I believe in confessing one's mistakes and correcting them. Such confession strengthens one and purifies the soul.

> Mohandas Karamchand (Mahatma) Gandhi

Dispossessing myself of all property has been a positive gain. I would like people to compete with me in my contentment. It is the richest treasure I own.

> Mohandas Karamchand (Mahatma) Gandhi

Ahimsa (infinite love) is a weapon of matchless potency. It is the *summum bonum* of life. It is an attribute of the brave, in fact it is their all. It does not come within the reach of the coward. It is no wooden or lifeless dogma, but a living and life giving force. It is the special attribute of the soul.

> Mohandas Karamchand (Mahatma) Gandhi

Man fools himself. He prays for a long life, yet fears an old age.

> Chinese Proverb

To be able under all circumstances to practice five things constitutes perfect virtue; these five are gravity, generosity of soul, sincerity, earnestness, and kindness.

> Confucius

When we see men of a contrary character, we should turn inwards and examine ourselves.

Confucius

The weak can never forgive. Forgiveness is an attribute of the strong.

Mohandas Karamchand (Mahatma) Gandhi

As human beings, our greatness lies not so much in being able to remake the world — that is the myth of the atomic age — as in being able to remake ourselves.

Mohandas Karamchand (Mahatma) Gandhi

On the stage of life, your part is just as important as anyone else's.

Paramahansa Yogananda

Wheresoever you go, go with all your heart.

Confucius

Be vigilant; guard your mind against negative thoughts.

Buddha

Goodness speaks in a whisper, evil shouts.

Tibetan Proverb

The opponents and I are really one. My strength and skills only half of the equation. The other half is theirs. An opponent is someone whose strength joined to yours creates a certain result.

Sadaharu Oh
Professional Baseball Player

In the practice of tolerance, one's enemy is the best teacher.

The Dalai Lama

I came after wandering from mountain to mountain.

"Have you reached the top?" asked the Master.

"Yes, I have reached it," answered the monk.

"Is there anyone there?" said the Master.

"No, no one is there," replied the monk.

"If so, it means that you have not yet reached the top," said the
Master.

"If I have not yet reached the top, how can I know there is no one there?" argued the monk.

"Then why don't you stay there?" said the Master.

Dongshan Liangjie

Those who, relying upon themselves only, not looking for assistance to anyone besides themselves, it is they who will reach the top-most height.

Buddha

Money gives you purchasing power, status gives you social power, but love and peace gives you the zest to live.

Kuldeep Gulati

Be truthful to yourself and truth will follow you.

Kuldeep Gulati

The gentleman is at ease without being arrogant; the small man is arrogant without being at ease.

Confucius

The most difficult battle you will ever face is the battle within yourself.

Zen Proverb

Don't you see, it really is an extraordinary thing that you are so afraid to be what you are, because that is where the beauty lies.

Jiddu Krishnamurti

Asian Words of Success

When you do something, you should burn yourself completely, like a good bonfire, leaving no trace of yourself.

Shunryū Suzuki

Never be satisfied. Never be bound by conventional wisdom.

Dr. Koichi Nishimura
CEO
Solectron Corp

Coming, going, the waterfowl leaves not a trace, nor does it need a guide.

Dōgen Zenji

Lifespan is measured in breaths, not years.

Hindu Proverb

What is needed, rather than running away or controlling or suppressing or any other resistance, is understanding fear; that means, watch it, learn about it, come directly into contact with it. We are to learn about fear, not how to escape from it.

Jiddu Krishnamurti

The difference between what we do and what we are capable of doing would suffice to solve most of the world's problems.

Mohandas Karamchand (Mahatma) Gandhi

Contemplate in the morning.
Pull weeds in the afternoon.
The joys and labor of a single day are part of a whole journey.

Tao Te Ching

If you love the sacred and despise the ordinary, you are still bobbing in the ocean of delusion.

Linji Yixuan

Therefore, be ye lamps unto yourselves, be a refuge to yourselves. Hold fast to Truth as a lamp; hold fast to the truth as a refuge. Look not for a refuge in anyone beside yourselves. And those, who shall be a lamp unto themselves, shall betake themselves to no external refuge, but holding fast to the Truth as their lamp, and holding fast to the Truth as their refuge, they shall reach the topmost Height.

Buddha

Old friends pass away, new friends appear. It is just like the days. An old day passes, a new day arrives. The important thing is to make it meaningful: a meaningful friend — or a meaningful day.

Dalai Lama

There is no fire like passion, there is no shark like hatred, there is no snare like folly, there is no torrent like greed.

Buddha

Even for our enemies in misery — there should be tears in our eyes.

Charan Singh

The effects of our actions may be postponed but they are never lost. There is an inevitable reward for good deeds and an inescapable punishment for bad. Reflect upon this truth, and seek always to earn good wages from destiny.

Wu Ming Fu

Knock on the sky and listen to the sound!

Zen Proverb

Enjoy yourself. It's later than you think.

Chinese Proverb

You yourself, as much as anybody in the entire universe, deserve your love and affection.

Buddha

A coward is incapable of exhibiting love, it is the prerogative of the brave.

Mohandas Karamchand (Mahatma) Gandhi

Asian Words of Success

The secret of health for both mind and body, is not to mourn for the past, not to worry about the future, not to anticipate troubles, but to live the present moment wisely and earnestly.

Buddha

Peace is not a relationship of nations. It is a condition of mind brought about by a serenity of soul. Lasting peace can come only to peaceful people.

Jawaharlal Nehru

Sometimes your joy is the source of your smile, but sometimes your smile can be the source of your joy.

Thich Nhat Hanh

Water which is too pure has no fish.

Ts'ai Ken T'an

Where there are humans you'll find flies, and Buddhas.

Kobayashi Issa

The purpose of our lives is to be happy.

Dalai Lama

If you can spend a perfectly useless afternoon in a perfectly useless manner, you have learned how to live.

Lin Yutang

Sit quietly, doing nothing, spring comes, and the grass grows by itself.

Zen Proverb

Life is so short we must move very slowly.

Thai Proverb

Whatever you do may seem insignificant to you, but it is most important that you do it.

Mohandas Karamchand (Mahatma) Gandhi

If you believe everything you read, you better not read.

Japanese Proverb

Neither fire nor wind, birth nor death can erase our good deeds.

Buddha

Life at any time can become difficult: life at any time can become easy. It all depends upon how one adjusts oneself to life.

Morarji Desai
India Prime Minister

The true test of one's character is how one handles adversity.

Wayne Cheng

Anger ends in cruelty.

Tamil Proverb

Help thy brother's boat across, and lo! — thine own has reached the shore.

Hindu Proverb

Prayer is not an old woman's idle amusement. Properly understood and applied, it is the most potent instrument of action.

Mohandas Karamchand (Mahatma) Gandhi

Work out your own salvation. Do not depend on others.

Buddha

The butterfly becomes only when it's entirely ready.

Chinese Proverb

To know the mind is the most important task of your life. And to know the mind is to know the world.

Buddhist Proverb

In the midst of great joy, do not promise anything. In the midst of great anger, do not answer anyone's letter.

Chinese Proverb

Asian Words of Success

Satisfaction lies in the effort, not in the attainment. Full effort is full victory.

> Mohandas Karamchand (Mahatma) Gandhi

Q: So how can I set myself free?
A: Who has bound you?

> Zen Kōan

The longer the night lasts, the more our dreams will be.
> Chinese Proverb

Every step I take in the light is mine forever.
> Swami Vivekananda

Choose a job you love and you will never have to work a day in your life.

> Confucius

He who knows others is clever. He who knows himself is enlightened.

> Lao-Tzu

Have a mouth as sharp as a dagger, but a heart as soft as tofu.
> Chinese Proverb

An inch of time is an inch of gold, but you can't buy that inch of time with an inch of gold.

Chinese Proverb

A smile will gain you ten more years of life.

Chinese Proverb

If you are patient in one moment of anger, you will escape a hundred days of sorrow.

Chinese Proverb

Sour, sweet, bitter, pungent, all must be tasted.

Chinese Proverb

When a finger points at the moon, the imbecile looks at the finger.

Chinese Proverb

Every day cannot be a feast of lanterns.

Chinese Proverb

I was angered, for I had no shoes. Then I met a man who had no feet.

Chinese Proverb

Asian Words of Success

The gods cannot help those who do not seize opportunities.

Chinese Proverb

There are a lot of valuable things in this world — property, possessions, work and so forth. But the most valuable thing is time. Like an arrow shot from a bow, it never returns. It is something you cannot hold onto, and it is impossible to recapture.

Kim Woo-Choong
Korean Entrepreneur

Only those who can be strict with themselves hold the key to coming out on top.

Umeo Oyama
Former Chairman
Tsugami Corporation

Dreams often make the person. They control your personality, your work, even your destiny. Dreams are like the rudder of a ship setting sail. The rudder may be small and unseen, but it controls the ship's course. So a life without dreams is like a ship without a rudder. Just as a ship without a rudder becomes nothing but a drifting craft, a person without a dream loses their direction and tosses about until they get caught in the seaweed.

Kim Woo-Choong
Korean Entrepreneur

To succeed in something, you must have capability but that capability alone is insufficient. In addition, you must have drive, concentration, and perseverance. Nothing is impossible, it is only your lack of tenacity that makes it seem impossible.

Toko Toshio
Japanese Entrepreneur

The human mind, when it is open, is capable of infinite growth. When it is closed, it shrivels and shrinks until ultimately it self destructs. The difference in that is enormous. The open, positive mind is capable of limitless wisdom and ingenuity. But the closed, shrunken mind produces nothing and leads only to failure.

Konosuke Matsushita

You need a pessimistic statement to remind us that not everything is rosy all the time. But the greater the challenge, the more creativity is released from the people.

Jose Almonte
Security Adviser to Philippine President Fidel Ramos

Realistic people are very limited. Realism is pessimism. Everything in the world can be changed by passion.

Imran Khan

Asian Words of Success

Teachers open the door, but you must enter by yourself.

Chinese Proverb

Virtue should be as common in the laborer as in the king.

Confucius

We are what we think. All that we are arises with our thoughts. With our thoughts, we make our world.

Buddha

Philosophy of the Ant? Hong Kong inhabitants say obstacles don't exist. Go around it, over it, under it, or through it but keep on going.

Hong Kong Philosophy

Those who cannot forgive others break the bridge over which they themselves must pass.

Confucius

If you always give you will always have.

Chinese Proverb

The miracle is not to fly in the air, or to walk on the water, but to walk on the earth.

Chinese Proverb

Concerning all acts of initiative (and creation), there is one elementary truth — that the moment one definitely commits oneself, then Providence moves too. All sorts of things occur to help one that would never otherwise have occurred. A whole stream of events issue from the decision, raising in one's favor all manner of unforeseen incidents and meetings and material assistance which no man could have dreamed would have come his way.

William Hutchinson Murray
(Leader Of Team That Scaled Mt. Everest)

The Master said, "Fine words and an insinuating appearance are seldom associated with true virtue."

Confucius

When the people of the world all know beauty as beauty, there arises the recognition of ugliness. When they all know the good as good, there arises the recognition of evil.

Lao-Tzu

The wise are free from perplexity, the virtuous are free from anxiety, the bold are free from fear.

Confucius

To talk goodness is not good. Only to do it is.

Chinese Proverb

Asian Words of Success

Great souls have wills; feeble ones have only wishes.

Chinese Proverb

Time spent laughing is time spent with the Gods.

Japanese Proverb

When you bow, bow low.

Chinese Proverb

Every man goes down to his death bearing in his hands only that which he has given away.

Persian Proverb

The best memory is that which forgets nothing, but injuries. Write kindness in marble and write injuries in the dust.

Persian Proverb

Those who know the truth are not equal to those who love it, and those who love it are not equal to those who live it.

Confucius

Don't be disquieted in time of adversity. Be firm with dignity and self-reliant with vigor.

Chiang Kai-shek

With virtue you cannot be entirely poor, without it you cannot be really rich.

Chinese Proverb

For him who has conquered the mind, the mind is the best of friends; but for one who has failed to do so, his mind will be the greatest enemy.

Bhagavad Gita

Every good act is charity. A man's true wealth hereafter is the good that he does in this world to his fellows.

Prophet Muhammad

Keep five yards from a carriage, ten yards from a horse, and a hundred yards from an elephant; but the distance one should keep from a wicked man cannot be measured.

Indian Proverb

To overcome evil with good is good, to resist evil by evil is evil.

Prophet Muhammad

Kindness in words creates confidence. Kindness in thinking creates profoundness. Kindness in giving creates love.

Lao-Tzu

Asian Words of Success

Acquire the courage to believe in yourself. Many of the things that you have been taught were at one time the radical ideas of individuals who had the courage to believe what their own hearts and minds told them was true, rather than accept the common beliefs of their day.

Ching Ning Chu

I am not concerned that I am not known, I seek to be worthy to be known.

Confucius

When with yourself watch your thoughts. When with others watch your speech.

Tibetan Proverb

The only tyrant I accept in this world is the 'still small voice' within me.

Mohandas Karamchand (Mahatma) Gandhi

You yourself are your own barrier. Rise from within it.

Rumi

A man is wealthy when he knows that he has enough.

Tibetan Proverb

Indolence is a delightful but distressing state; we must be doing something to be happy.

Mohandas Karamchand (Mahatma) Gandhi

To give pleasure to a single heart by a single act is better than a thousand heads bowing in prayer.

Mohandas Karamchand (Mahatma) Gandhi

There is no greater injury to one's character than practicing virtue with ulterior motivation.

Chuang Tzu

There is nothing noble about being superior to some other men. The true nobility is in being superior to your previous self.

Hindu Proverb

When you are inspired by some great purpose, some extraordinary project, all of your thoughts break their bonds: your mind transcends limitations, your consciousness expands in every direction and you find yourself in a new, great, and wonderful world. Dormant forces, faculties, and talents become alive and you discover yourself to be a greater person than you ever dreamed yourself to be.

Patañjali

Ordinary men hate solitude. But the Master makes use of it, embracing his aloneness, realizing he is one with the whole universe.

Lao-Tzu

To believe in something, and not to live it, is dishonest.

Mohandas Karamchand (Mahatma) Gandhi

People deal too much with the negative, with what is wrong. Why not try and see positive things, to just touch those things and make them bloom?

Thich Nhat Hanh

To understand anything is to find in it something which is our own, and it is the discovery of ourselves outside us which makes us glad.

Rabindranath Tagore

When you are content to be simply yourself and don't compare or compete, everyone will respect you.

Lao-Tzu

There are two perfect men: one dead and the other unborn.

Chinese Proverb

Ever since man began to till the soil and learned not to eat the seed grain, but to plant it and wait for the harvest, the postponement of gratification has been the basis of a higher standard of living and civilization.

Samuel Ichiye Hayakawa

It ill becomes us to invoke in our daily prayers the blessing of God, the Compassionate, if we in turn will not practice elementary compassion towards our fellow creatures.

Mohandas Karamchand (Mahatma) Gandhi

The worthy person, by being enlightened, enlightens others. Today people, being bewildered, bewilder others.

Mencius

The more you know, the less you understand.

Lao-Tzu

Which does one love more, fame or one's own life? Which is more valuable, one's own life or wealth? Which is worse, gain or loss? Therefore he who has lavish desires will spend extravagantly. He who hoards most will lose heavily. He who is contented suffers no disgrace. He who knows when to stop is free from danger. Therefore he can long endure.

Lao-Tzu

Asian Words of Success

The mind that turns forever outward will have no end to craving. Only the mind turned inward will find a still-point of peace.

Tao Te Ching

He who possesses the source of enthusiasm will achieve great things.

I Ching

Indecision regarding the choice among pleasures temporarily robs a man of inner peace. After due reflection, he attains joy by turning away from the lower pleasures and seeking the higher ones.

I Ching

No one can see their reflection in running water. It is only in still water that we can see.

Taoist Proverb

Any man who strives to do his best, whether his work be great or small, is considered to be doing the work of a lion.

Nagarjuna

Be a lamp unto yourself.

Buddha

You must be still in the midst of activity, and be vibrantly alive in repose.

Indira Gandhi

If you want others to be happy, practice compassion. If you want to be happy, practice compassion.

Dalai Lama

The sages do not consider that making no mistakes is a blessing. They believe, rather, that the great virtue of man lies in his ability to correct his mistakes and continually make a new man of himself.

Wang Yangming

This is my simple religion. There is no need for temples; no need for complicated philosophy. Our own brain, our own heart is our temple; the philosophy is kindness.

Dalai Lama

It is not how much you do, but how much love you put in the doing.

Mother Teresa

That the birds of worry and care fly over your head, this you cannot change, but that they build nests in your hair, this you can prevent.

Chinese Proverb

Truth comes as conqueror only to those who have lost the art of receiving it as a friend.

Rabindranath Tagore

It is man that makes truth great, not truth that makes man great.

Confucius

There are three sorts of friend that are profitable, and three sorts that are harmful. Friendship with the upright, with the true-to-death and with those who have heard much is profitable. Friendship with the obsequious, with those who are good at accommodating their principles, or those who are clever at talk is harmful.

Confucius

When you have only two pennies left in the world, buy a loaf of bread with one, and a lily with the other.

Chinese Proverb

Asian Words of Success

To receive everything, one must open one's hands and give.

Taisen Deshimaru

Your own self is your ultimate teacher (*sadguru*). The outer teacher (guru) is merely a milestone. It is only your inner teacher that will walk with you to the goal, for he is the goal.

Nisargadatta Maharaj

Most people give in to their baser instincts, thinking more of short-term pleasures and gains than the kind of sustained self-restraint required in order to practice what is good and reject what is bad.

Datuk Seri Dr Mahathir Mohamad
Malaysia Prime Minister

A bird does not sing because it has an answer; it sings because it has a song.

Chinese Proverb

The Zen "genius" sleeps in every one of us and demands an awakening.

D.T. Suzuki

Doubt everything. Find your own light.

Lao-Tzu

The true teacher has no students — all is being and only silence speaks. The perfect teacher has no teachings because he knows that you are free already. So the true teacher's non-teaching is that there is no teacher, no student, no teaching and that nothing has ever existed. This teaching must be without words and must land in your heart. If you try to understand it, it will only land in your head.

Hariwansh Lal (Papaji) Poonja

Self-help must precede help from others.

Morarji Desai

Guru is not the physical form. So the contact will remain even after the physical form of the Guru vanishes. One can go to another Guru after one's Guru passes away, but all Gurus are one and none of them is the form you see. Always mental contact is the best.

Ramana Maharshi

The true Teacher removes all names and forms and concepts. The preacher adds them like a noose around your neck. The preacher clings to you like a vulture clings to a fresh corpse. The True Teacher will teach only to the extent that can be absorbed and then send the student away.

Hariwansh Lal (Papaji) Poonja

When you reach the top, keep climbing.

Zen Proverb

Live as if you were to die tomorrow. Learn as if you were to live forever.

Mohandas Karamchand (Mahatma) Gandhi

Learning is weightless, a treasure you can always carry easily.

Chinese Proverb

Look for the answer inside your question.

Rumi

The key to growth is the introduction of higher dimensions of consciousness into our awareness.

Lao-Tzu

Manifest plainness,
Embrace simplicity,
Reduce selfishness,
Have few desires.

Buddha's last words
(in Theravada tradition)

Miso with the smell of miso is not good miso. Enlightenment with the smell of enlightenment is not the real enlightenment.

Zen Proverb

Asian Words of Success

Don't be disquieted in time of adversity. Be firm with dignity and self-reliant with vigor.

Chiang Kai-shek

He is poor who does not feel content.

Japanese Proverb

Asian Words of Success

Continuous Learning

Continuous learning is a crucial process for personal and professional success. Both organizations and individuals have a need for continuous learning.

On an organizational level, the core competencies required for success in today's highly competitive marketplaces include leadership, teamwork, innovation, leading change, vision alignment, and optimizing cross-functional performance. No one is born with enough natural skills in all these areas. Thus, it is the responsibility of the senior management team to recruit, develop, and promote these competencies within the organization.

Many companies do not leverage the great diversities of culture found within their organizations to drive value, even those which operate across borders and continents. This is both sad and surprising, since almost all large organizations today have cross-border operations, market their products and services in numerous countries, or have multinational workforces.

Cultural inclusiveness is not a passing fad. Understanding cultural biases and preferences is critical for leaders, especially those who lead individuals and teams in remote locations and different countries. A leader's ability to understand naturally diverse approaches to work, interpersonal communications, hierarchical respect, and other cultural norms will directly impact the success of any cross-border strategy implementation.

The process for leading individuals and teams with cultural awareness and sensitivity is fairly easy to understand. But first it takes exposure to the biases and preferences found in other cultures and how these might impact the leader's ability to successfully lead. Assuredly, cross-cultural awareness and understanding requires continuous learning on both a professional and personal basis.

On the individual level, people are seeking new insights on a wide spectrum of topics, ranging from parenting skills to self-development, and from personal interests and hobbies to in-depth knowledge on specific pursuits.

It is little wonder, therefore, that we see so many adults seeking formal or informal education well after their official schooling years are over. This also explains why training and education continue to be growth industries, even during times of economic downturns.

The desire for continuous learning goes back to the very earliest days of civilization. One might even argue that learning was one of the pillars that helped mankind enter the arena of civilization.

In Japan, the concept of **kaizen**, or continuous improvement, is deeply embedded in the corporate cultures of the most successful Japanese firms. Years ago this author began to apply the concept of **kaizen** to my own personal and professional lives, and each month I continue to rigorously look at ways to improve myself in the ten areas I deem most important to me.

Fortunately, it is easy and free to engage in continuous learning today, with so much information available via the Internet, including full college courses. Plus, there are a number of learning sites such as Udemy, YouTube, iTunesU, Coursera, Udacity, and the Khan Academy providing structured lessons and "how to" videos. There is really no excuse today for anyone to ever stop learning.

I hope the quotes and phrases in this section motivate you to increase your own personal commitment to continuous learning in the areas most important to you, and that this section will bring the spirit of **kaizen** into your life and, if you are the leader of an organization or a group, into that entity as well.

A single conversation across the table with a wise man is worth a month's study of books.

Chinese Proverb

Better than a thousand days of diligent study is one day with a great teacher.

Japanese Proverb

To be fond of learning is to be near knowledge.

Confucius

When the student is ready, the master appears.

Buddhist Proverb

The function of education is to eradicate, inwardly as well as outwardly, the fear that destroys human thought, human relationship, and love.

Jiddu Krishnamurti

So when you are listening to somebody, completely, attentively, then you are listening not only to the words, but also to the feeling of what is being conveyed, to the whole of it, not part of it.

Jiddu Krishnamurti

Let a hundred flowers blossom, and let a hundred schools of thought contend.

Mao Zedong

A book is a garden carried in the pocket.

Chinese Proverb

Think of experience as something divine; we teach based on experience. Experience allows us to speak with authority. You must trust experience as something divine.

Awa Kenzo

Find a teacher who is an integral being, a beacon who extends his light and virtue with equal ease to those who appreciate him and those who don't. Shape yourself in his mold, bathe in his nourishing radiance, and reflect it out to the rest of the world.

Lao-Tzu

Asian Words of Success

At 15, I set my heart upon learning.

At 30, I planted my feet firm upon the ground.

At 40, I no longer suffered from perplexities.

At 50, I knew what were the biddings of Heaven.

At 60, I heard them with docile ear.

At 70, I could follow the dictates of my own heart; for what I
desired no longer overstepped the boundaries of right.

> Confucius

By three methods we may learn wisdom: First, by reflection, which is noblest; second, by imitation, which is easiest; and third, by experience, which is the bitterest.

> Confucius

A book holds a house of gold.

> Chinese Proverb

Those who do not read are no better off than those who cannot.

> Chinese Proverb

Be not afraid of growing slowly; be afraid only of standing still.

> Chinese Proverb

One pound of learning requires ten pounds of common sense to apply it.

Persian Proverb

We live in the present, we dream of the future, but we learn eternal truths from the past.

Madame Chiang Kai-shek

Believe nothing merely because you have been told it. Do not believe what your teacher tells you merely out of respect for the teacher. But whatsoever, after due examination and analysis, you find to be kind, conducive to the good, the benefit, the welfare of all beings — that doctrine believe and cling to, and take it as your guide.

Buddha

Business is also cultural and communication biased, and communication is 75 percent non-verbal. In fact, emotional communication is 90 percent non-verbal, therefore only first-hand learning in Asia teaches us how to take action, and gain cooperation from others to achieve results.

Dr Wong Yip Yan
Founder and Chairman
The WyWy Group of Companies

Ever climbing, ever reaching. Ever striving, ever surpassing. Ever gaining, ever accumulating. For leaders these alone are the ways to attain. And so for fifty years or more they repeat the pattern until stopped by circumstances, by disillusion, or by death.

Lao-Tzu

We will bring about a mindset change among Singaporeans. We must get away from the idea that it is only the people at the top who should be thinking, and the job of everyone else is to do as told. Instead we want to bring about a spirit of innovation, of learning by doing, of everyone each at his own level all the time asking how he can do his job better.

Goh Chok Tong
Singapore Prime Minister

What does a company have to do to ensure that it does not degenerate — and eventually die? It just has to take up new challenges regardless of the difficulties, to have the free spirit of an entrepreneur. Its people should even be a little impulsive, but should not make the same mistakes twice. If people did that, the company safe would soon be empty.

Seiichi Takikawa
Chairman and CEO
Canon Sales Co

First, I ask everybody to make today better than yesterday, then make tomorrow better than today. This is what we call kaizen. Second, as the head of the enterprise, I must lead the way by personally being creative and encouraging others to follow. Third, I pay special attention to make sure such efforts continue every day, incessantly, 365 days a year. Finally, I avoid looking for a magical "quick fix" that will make the company grow. Instead, I try to rely on daily innovative efforts to develop the enterprise naturally.

Kazuo Inamori
Founder and Chairman
Kyocera Corporation and DDI Corporation

It is no longer enough to reprocess ideas from other parts of the world. Asian firms must learn to originate ideas themselves.

John Kao
Academic Director / Managing Innovation Program
Stanford University

The world is changing minute by minute. A company alone is not allowed to enjoy stability. If it puts too much emphasis on being stable, it won't be able to keep up with the times and will go bankrupt.

Koji Kobayashi
Chairman
NEC Corporation

A nation's wealth in the 21st century will depend on the capacity of its people to learn. Their ability to seek out new technologies and ideas — and to apply them — will be the key source of economic growth.

Goh Chok Tong
Singapore Prime Minister

No country can stand still. We have to keep upgrading and it gets harder as you go up.

Amnuay Viravan
Thailand Deputy PM and Finance Minister

To constantly stay ahead of the competition, businesses must keep innovating. IT has enabled many of the changes that are now possible. In the past our challenge was to make technology work for the business. Today it is deciding how to use technology to change business.

Willie Cheng
Managing Partner
Anderson Consulting

The whole secret of existence is to have no fear. Never fear what will become of you; depend on no one. Only the moment you reject all help are you freed.

Buddha

If one learns from others but does not think, one will be bewildered. If, on the other hand, one thinks but does not learn from others, one will be in peril.

Confucius

The difficulty in the spiritual path is always what comes from ourselves. A person does not like to be a pupil, he likes to be a teacher. If one only knew that the greatness and perfection of the great ones who have come from time to time to this world was in their being pupils and not in teaching! The greater the teacher, the better pupil he was. He learned from everyone, the great and the lowly, the wise and the foolish, the old and the young. He learned from their lives, and studied human nature in all its aspects.

Inayat Khan

Even when walking in the company of two other men, I am bound to be able to learn from them. The good points of one I copy; the bad points of the other I correct in myself.

Confucius

While heeding the profit of my counsel, avail yourself also of any helpful circumstances over and beyond the ordinary rules.

Sun Tzu

Asian Words of Success

When knowledge is extended, the will becomes sincere.
When the will is sincere, the mind is correct.
When the mind is correct, the self is cultivated.
When the self is cultivated, the clan is harmonized.
When the clan is harmonized, the country is well governed.
When the country is well governed, there will be peace through the land.

Confucius

There are many paths to enlightenment. Be sure to take one with a heart.

Lao-Tzu

The beginning of wisdom is to call things by their right names.

Chinese Proverb

He who conquers the mind, conquers the world.

Paramahansa Yogananda

Action should culminate in wisdom.

Bhagavad Gita

All that we are is the result of what we have thought.

Buddha

Asian Words of Success

In studying the way, realizing it is hard. Once you have realized it, preserving it is hard. When you can preserve it, putting it into practice is hard.

Zen Proverb

Success is 99 percent failure.

Soichiro Honda
Founder
Honda Motor Corporation

The words of truth are always paradoxical.

Lao-Tzu

Freedom is not worth having if it does not include the freedom to make mistakes.

Mohandas Karamchand (Mahatma) Gandhi

When your thinking rises above concern for your own welfare, wisdom which is independent of thought appears.

Hagakure

To teach is to learn.

Japanese Proverb

The palest ink is better than the best memory.

Chinese Proverb

Great undertakings cannot succeed during periods of division and mutual alienation. The superior man recognizes the circumstances, does not become impatient, and sets about achieving gradual improvements in small matters.

I Ching

To understand your parents' love, bear your own children.

Chinese Proverb

Real knowledge is to know the extent of one's ignorance.

Confucius

When you know a thing, to recognize that you know it, and when you do not know a thing, to recognize that you do not know it. That is knowledge.

Confucius

Learning is like rowing upstream; not to advance is to drop back.

Chinese Proverb

Put away the book, the description, the tradition, the authority, and take the journey of self-discovery.

Jiddu Krishnamurti

Learning without thought is labor lost. Thought without learning is perilous.

Confucius

He who pursues learning will increase every day. He who pursues Tao will decrease every day.

Lao-Tzu

A cultured person is fond of learning and is not ashamed to ask questions of those beneath him.

Confucius
Analects

The man who puts great emphasis on exercising his mind is the man who fully understands his true nature.

Confucius

Asian Words of Success

Miscellaneous

To be idle is a short road to death and to be diligent is a way of life; foolish people are idle, wise people are diligent.

Buddha

There are seven things that will destroy us: Wealth without work; Pleasure without conscience; Knowledge without character; Religion without sacrifice; Politics without principle; Science without humanity; Business without ethics.

Mohandas Karamchand (Mahatma) Gandhi

They cannot take away our self-respect if we do not give it to them.

Mohandas Karamchand (Mahatma) Gandhi

When I despair, I remember that all through history the way of truth and love has always won. There have been tyrants and murderers and for a time they seem invincible but in the end, they always fall — think of it, ALWAYS.

Mohandas Karamchand (Mahatma) Gandhi

I pray for a more friendly, more caring, and more understanding human family on this planet. To all who dislike suffering, who cherish lasting happiness, this is my heartfelt appeal.

Dalai Lama

The universe operates through dynamic exchange....giving and receiving are different aspects of the flow of energy in the universe. And in our willingness to give that which we seek, we keep the abundance of the universe circulating in our lives.

Deepak Chopra

If we are to teach real peace in this world, and if we are to carry on a real war against war, we shall have to begin with the children.

Mohandas Karamchand (Mahatma) Gandhi

What the world wants is character. The world is in need of those whose life is one burning love, selfless.

Swami Vivekananda

Truth is indestructible, virtue is indestructible, purity is indestructible.

Swami Vivekananda

Asian Words of Success

Even a hare will bite when it is cornered.

Chinese Proverb

Innovation is essential to life, and it is not as hard as you might think. The problem is not the innovation itself, but whether or not you want to innovate.

Kim Woo-Choong
Korean Entrepreneur

In the information age that we are living in, the Malaysian society must be information rich. It can be no accident that there is today no wealthy, developed country that is information-poor and no information-rich country that is poor and underdeveloped.

Datuk Seri Dr Mahathir Mohamad
Malaysia Prime Minister

Each one has to find his peace from within. And peace to be real must be unaffected by outside circumstances.

Mohandas Karamchand (Mahatma) Gandhi

A fractious nation, like a broken rice-bowl, will not be able to feed its people.

Goh Chok Tong
Singapore Prime Minister

Asian Words of Success

Peace proposals unaccompanied by a sworn covenant indicate a plot.

Sun Tzu

The blind person never fears ghosts.

Burmese Proverb

If you are poor, though you dwell in the busy marketplace, no one will inquire about you; if you are rich, though you dwell in the heart of the mountains, you will have distant relatives.

Chinese Proverb

In matters of conscience, the law of majority has no place.

Mohandas Karamchand (Mahatma) Gandhi

Better never to have met you in my dream than to wake and reach for hands that are not there.

Ōtomo no Yakamochi

We think that the best kind of dialogue is one where both sides are able to put forward their hopes, their fears, their aspirations, what they would like, what they would not like, then find a solution acceptable to both sides — which must be a solution that is best for the country as a whole.

Aung San Suu Kyi

I tried to find Him on the Christian cross, but He was not there; I went to the temple of the Hindus and to the old pagodas, but I could not find a trace of Him anywhere. I searched on the mountains and in the valleys, but neither in the heights nor in the depths was I able to find Him. I went to the Kaaba in Mecca, but He was not there either. I questioned the scholars and philosophers, but He was beyond their understanding. I then looked into my heart and it was there where He dwelled that I saw Him; He was nowhere else to be found.

Rumi

The world we must strive to build needs to be based on the concept of genuine social equality — in it, the prince and the peasant, the wealthy and the less well-off, the employer and the employee are on the same level. Economic progress cannot mean that few people charge ahead and more and more people are left behind.

Mohandas Karamchand (Mahatma) Gandhi

The infinite is the finite of every instant.

Zen Proverb

Nature is not human-hearted.

Lao-Tzu

I have not the qualifications for teaching my philosophy on life. I have barely qualifications for practicing the philosophy I believe. I am but a poor struggling soul yearning to be wholly truthful and wholly non-violent in thought, word and deed, but ever failing to reach the ideal.

Mohandas Karamchand (Mahatma) Gandhi

The smile that flickers on baby's lips when he sleeps; does anybody know where it was born? Yes, there is a rumor that a young pale beam of a crescent moon touched the edge of a vanishing autumn cloud, and there the smile was first born.

Rabindranath Tagore

An eye for an eye leaves everyone blind.

Mohandas Karamchand (Mahatma) Gandhi

Every truth in this world has its opposite somewhere.

U Nu

Do not say, "It is morning," and dismiss it with a name of yesterday. See it for the first time as a new-born child that has no name.

Rabindranath Tagore

Know thou the self (spirit) as riding in a chariot, the body as the chariot. Know thou the intellect as the chariot-driver, and the mind as the reins. The senses, they say, are the horses; the objects of sense, what they range over. The self, combined with senses and mind, Wise Men call "the enjoyer."

Upanishads

The first principle of nonviolent action is that of non-cooperation with everything humiliating.

Mohandas Karamchand (Mahatma) Gandhi

Do not close your eyes before suffering. Find ways to be with those who are suffering by all means, including personal contacts and visits. By such means awaken yourself and others to the realities of suffering in the world.

Buddha

Faith is the bird that feels the light and sings when the dawn is still dark.

Rabindranath Tagore

No culture can live, if it attempts to be exclusive.

Mohandas Karamchand (Mahatma) Gandhi

Asian Words of Success

I will not let anyone walk through my mind with their dirty feet.

> Mohandas Karamchand (Mahatma) Gandhi

Honest disagreement is often a good sign of progress.

> Mohandas Karamchand (Mahatma) Gandhi

In focal ground, I would strengthen my alliance.

> Sun Tzu

Friendship is one mind in two bodies.

> Mencius

I see true innovation to be made up of three key elements which I call "the three creativities." Creativity in technology, of course, plus creativity in product planning, and marketing as well.

> Akio Morita
> Chairman
> Sony Corporation

A good traveler has no fixed plans and is not intent upon arriving.

> Lao-Tzu

Asian Words of Success

There is no doubt that world-class companies have reached their position because of their ability to innovate. For some companies, innovation has led to their gaining a greater share of the market. For others, it's either innovate or perish. What we need is not just one bright idea, but one bright idea after another. More importantly, new products and services must go into the market ahead of competition. To stay ahead, Singapore companies must have thinking employees. They must reward innovators. But they must be prepared to take risks, and accept the occasional failure.

Lim Boon Heng
Singapore Minister Without Portfolio
Chairman Singapore Productivity and Standards Board

It takes about 500 ideas to be generated for even one innovation to come to fruition.

Kenichi Ohmae

Alliances make an army strong.

Sun Tzu

Do not wait for leaders. Do it alone, person to person.

Mother Theresa

The best politics is right action.

Mohandas Karamchand (Mahatma) Gandhi

No one can guarantee the definite success of a new product introduction. On the other hand, without regular introduction of innovative products and services, long-term survival is doubtful for any company. The key to success for entrepreneurial companies and individuals is to be proactive and adaptive in introducing new innovations and not to fear failure, but to move on despite failure. To do nothing for fear of failure is failure already.

Bob Foo

The mind seeks continuous improvement to the quality of life through imagination and creativity. When innovation stops, so does growth.

Amirsham A Aziz
Managing Director
Malayan Banking Berhad

You have to break down the "silos" that separate one department from another so that people can cooperate. When people are equally accountable, they can achieve great things. The threads that form individual talent become bound together to form a rope that can pull the company to the top.

Y.S Kim
Chief Executive Officer
AST Research

But in the end, it will still be people — working together creatively — who will make the most important decisions, who will make the big difference. Information Technology will work. Information Technology will help advance Philippine progress vigorously — and this will be limited only by the extent to which we ourselves work productively, and help each other for our people's benefit.

Fidel V. Ramos
Philippine President

There is no essential difference between the manager and the employee. It's not the kind of relationship where one employs and the other is employed. People who trust one another get together to work for a team called a company, which I regard as a community that shares the same destiny. We are the partners that can trust one another, and I am the leader of that mutually loving pack.

Kazuo Inamori
Chairman and Founder
Kyocera Corporation

What we are doing to the forests of the world is but a mirror reflection of what we are doing to ourselves and to one another.

Mohandas Karamchand (Mahatma) Gandhi

The first prerequisite for a strong enterprise is teamwork or harmony among the people. I always compare the executive staff to a rugby football team. The president, executive vice president, and managing directors form the first row of the scrum, and executive directors and their subordinates form the second and third rows. How the forward heels out the ball will determine the development of the game.

Ichiro Inumaru
President
The Imperial Hotel

One person can have a lot of ideas and innovations. But without the teamwork to follow through, these can't be implemented.

Stan Shih
CEO
Acer Group

About the Author

Steven Howard
Global Leadership Development and Facilitation
Leadership Coach | Keynote Speaker

Steven Howard specializes in creating and delivering Leadership Development curriculum for frontline leaders, mid-level leaders, senior leaders and high-potential leaders.

An author with 36 years of international senior sales, marketing, and leadership experience, his corporate career covered a wide variety of fields and experiences, including Regional Marketing Director for Texas Instruments Asia-Pacific, South Asia & ASEAN Regional Director for TIME Magazine, Global Account Director at BBDO Advertising handling an international airline account, and VP Marketing for Citibank's Consumer Banking Group.

Since 1988 he has delivered leadership development training programs in the U.S., Asia, Australia, Africa, Canada, and Europe to numerous organizations, including Citicorp, Covidien, DBS Bank, Deutsche Bank, DuPont Lycra, Esso Productions, ExxonMobil, Hewlett Packard Enterprise,

Micron Technology, Motorola Solutions, SapientNitro, Standard Chartered Bank, and many others.

He has been a member of the training faculty at MasterCard University Asia/Pacific, the Citibank Asia-Pacific Banking Institute, and Forum Corporation. He brings a truly international, cross-cultural perspective to his leadership development programs, having lived in the USA for 26 years, in Singapore for 21 years and in Australia for 12 years.

In addition to his leadership facilitation work Steven has served on several Boards in both the private and non-profit sectors. He has also chaired a strategic advisory group for a local government entity and a national sporting organization that is a member of the Australian Olympic Committee.

Steven is the author of 16 marketing, management, and leadership books and is the editor of three professional and personal development books in the *Project You* series.

His books are:

> **Corporate Image Management:** *A Marketing Discipline*

> **Powerful Marketing Minutes:** *50 Ways to Develop Market Leadership*

> **MORE Powerful Marketing Minutes:** *50 New Ways to Develop Market Leadership*

Asian Words of Wisdom

Asian Words of Knowledge

Essential Asian Words of Wisdom

Pillars of Growth: *Strategies for Leading Sustainable Growth* (co-author with three others)

Motivation Plus Marketing Equals Money (co-author with four others)

Marketing Words of Wisdom

The Best of the Monday Morning Marketing Memo

Powerful Marketing Memos

8 Keys To Becoming A Great Leader *(With Leadership Lessons and Tips from Gibbs, Yoda and Capt'n Jack Sparrow)*

Asian Words of Success

Asian Words of Meaning

Asian Words of Inspiration

The Book of Asian Proverbs

Contact Details

Email: steven@CalienteLeadership.com

Twitter: @stevenbhoward | @GreatLeadershp

LinkedIn: www.linkedin.com/in/stevenbhoward

Facebook: www.facebook.com/CalienteLeadership

Website: www.CalienteLeadership.com

Blog: CalienteLeadership.com/TheArtofGreatLeadershipBlog

Reader Reviews Appreciated

Thank you for reading this book. I hope you found some useful nuggets of wisdom that are relevant to your current and future life journey.

One favor to ask, if I may. Please take a few minutes, go to this book's page on Amazon and leave a reader review. Here's the link: http://www.amazon.com/dp/B01LM0K8BM.

As an author I sincerely appreciate hearing from my readers. And I know other readers often use these reviews in determining whether a book might meet their needs.

Thank you in advance.

And best wishes for continued success in your professional and personal endeavors.

Asian Words of Success

www.ingramcontent.com/pod-product-compliance
Lightning Source LLC
Chambersburg PA
CBHW060443040426
42331CB00044B/2530